What Do You Bring to the Table?

*A Savory, Sensory and Inspirational Guide
to Living a Yummy Delicious Life*

Written with *love*
by
Shelley Whizin

A Happy Mindful Cook

Founder of the Soul Diving Institute

Editor: Marie Louise Zervos

Photographer : Delaram Pourabdi

Lighthearts Publishing Company

Los Angeles, California

Library of Congress Cataloging-in-Publication Data

Whizin, Shelley.
What Do You Bring to the Table? A Sensory, Savory and Inspirational Guide to Living a Yummy Delicious Life. – 1st Ed.
ISBN: 978-1-68007-075-0
1st Edition, November 2020
Printed in the United States of America
For inquiries and to order additional copies; go to amazon.com

This book is dedicated to my beautiful family,

My daughter, Sarah

My son-in-law Mike

My grandchildren, Jake, Jordyn & Zoe

May this be the beginning of many words to come…

Endorsements

*"After reading **What Do You Bring to the Table?** I learned the meaning of living your life from the inside out. I can now take this learning and apply it to my relationships, my job and the way I treat myself. Using cooking as an analogy for life brings a unique approach because it engages your whole body – heart and mind. I found it especially helpful to take a few moments to do the Happy Mindful Meditations prior to cooking, and I also do them at any other time to tap into the way my entire body feels. As a person who has struggled with anxiety and panic attacks since I was a child, I found that the Meditations were incredibly helpful. Furthermore, these Mediations serve as key additions to my arsenal of daily practices that help with my overall well-being and are great for helping me ground myself. This book is one that I would give as a gift to my friends and family. Although it's a self-help book in many ways, it's also a book that can bring families together by stimulating discussion and mindfulness. It promotes human understanding with kindness, fostering a deeper conscientious awareness – even a renewed commitment, of how important it is to own taking quality time with one another in a healthy way. The book is deeply meaningful treat for the senses, and food for the soul."*

-Emily Stoltzman, Make-up Artist

"Shelley has been hugely instrumental in helping me achieve a deep understanding of some key aspects leading to my personal growth and metanoia transformation. Her book, **What Do You Bring to the Table?** *speaks to me in a way that has also helped and prepared me for what I am about to give and receive. I feel extremely confident that you will find her book enjoyable. It's informative, interactive and challenges you to find your spiritual purpose and have a better understanding of what you bring to the table."*

-Daniel Meyers, CBO, Chief Baby Officer, Ebaby.com

"When I heard that Shelley was putting out a cookbook that combined food with her wise teachings on BEing human, I knew it would be a hit. Through her words, Shelley Whizin exemplifies kindness, forgiveness, joy, and love for all, using cooking recipes not only to feed the body, but more importantly to encourage an awareness of soul nurturing. As a recipient of her friendship and a learner of all she teaches, I have witnessed, celebrated and enjoyed all Shelley brings to the table, and not just with food which defines 'yummy delicious', but also to the table of life!!! This book serves food for thought on a platter of love."

– Jill Schoelen, Actress, Singer, Producer

"Shelley Whizin's book, **What Do You Bring to the Table?** *is spot on in its messages, and there are many helpful insights I got in reading her book. These have helped me remove stress, be more conscious of coming from compassion, caring, love, and joy. It brought me a renewed conscientiousness in sharing – no matter how simple the recipe may be, and the deep breathing in the Happy Mindful Meditations brought renewed importance for me.* This book is a Covid-19 Survival Guide, and it has helped me focus on my life not Covid. *I'm more aware every day now of what I bring to the table of life, and cook delicious, healthy food with Love. Thanks, Shelley".*

-Sam Herr, Retired Restaurateur, Chief Food Preparer

"What Do You Bring to the Table?*" is about understanding and appreciating life's basics through the analogy of cooking - you get what you put in. Shelley's book gives valuable insights on how to live life, and her wise approach guides us on how to be the best version of ourselves. This cookbook is a spiritual journey by itself, and I enjoyed it very much. Shelley's teachings can definitely be life-changing!*

-Darsweil Rogers, Co-Managing Partner CFP Innovation, Radio Talk Show Host

Contents

Acknowledgements

There are always many people to acknowledge in life, for we stand tall on those who came before us to guide us in many ways, and thus we are never alone in what we do. I am fortunate to have crossed paths with a wide range of extraordinary people along my life's journey who have auspiciously held significant roles in helping me find my life's calling, activating and expanding me to manifest my deepest desires/ gifts/talents. Each of these persons believed in me and supported me, even in times when I didn't believe so much in myself. I am deeply grateful for each and every one of these remarkable individuals who has encouraged me, found value in my teachings and has fostered my expansion with their belief in my life's purpose.

Whether any of my friends, acquaintances, teachers, and others may not be acknowledged by name here, each one knows who he/she is. I'd like to say that each and every one, always holds a special place in my heart. I am so blessed to have been able to meet each one in this life, study with some of you in person, and know others through their courses, books and lectures. A big thank you to all those who have contributed to my life's journey.

I have to now say that I feel that I am the luckiest mom and grandma, aka "Nooni", in the whole wide world. With deep love I feel blessed and forever grateful for my beautiful, resourceful, thoughtful and loving daughter, Sarah Schultz, and for my special son-in-law Mike who is Sarah's wonderful high-school-sweetheart-husband.

He is such a fine human being and a devoted father. I feel blessed to have three beautiful, bright, inquisitive and spirited grandchildren, Jake, Jordyn, and Zoe, all whom I love beyond words. "You are all my constant inspiration. How fortunate am I to have you as my family. I learn from you, and I'm am grateful that you're always open to learn from me too. I just love watching you all grow!" 🙏

I have forever been transformed, changed and expanded beyond measure by my life steward, and mentor, Marie Louise Zervos. Brilliant and beautiful, she is also the editor par excellence of all of my writings! I am truly blessed to also count her as a beloved friend for life. Over many years I still continue to draw deep, boundless growth from her excellent life guidance, stewardship, and mentorship, that continue to bring out all the facets that are authentically me. Innumerable aspects and depths of these have all shaped and molded who I am and what I represent today. I just feel deep gratitude for everything she's done to bring me to discover my life's purpose. Her creative content contribution to this book has been truly significant, and I credit her as well for the design and structure of this book giving it its original style. I love how she always lassoes my energy turning so much of it into words that are exceptionally articulate, exact, easily digestible and helpful to others. "Thank you so very much, dear Marie Louise, for guiding my heart and soul to heal from many childhood wounds. I'll also never forget that you saved me after a 6-year hiatus of putting my own self aside to give devoted help to my beautiful friends, Toni and Gene Bua, before each passed into the light. Powerfully intuitive, you scooped me up in that huge energy of yours to guide me anew to reclaim my me, my life and purpose. Without you, Marie Louise, this book would not have been possible. Thank you, beyond words, for your unfaltering, constant belief in me, and for your extraordinary guidance with exceptional encouragement over all these years to write a book." 🙏

There is no way I could utter one more word without thanking my dear friend, Sima Cohen. Sima exudes a big fireball of energy and she is a woman that has lit up my heart-light with sparks of excitement! Sima herself has published a cookbook called, "Sima's Healthy Indulgence". She has served as an inspiration, further fueled our common love of conscientious eating and living. She's played a remarkable role in making my own book, "What Do You Bring to the Table", become a reality. "Sima, I am absolutely delighted and forever blessed that you popped into my life. By nature of this book I'm grateful you prodded me into having a social media presence, encouraging me to talk more, produce videos and share with the world my love of cooking lovingly peppered with wisdoms. Thank you for being so selflessly sharing of yourself with me. Thank you for sharing your media experiences with me, and as well your time. As my friend for life, fellow soul diver, and perpetual student of the human/spiritual dynamic, you are deeply appreciated. Thank you for letting me into your heart." 🙏

My life is so much more enriched for knowing my dear, delightfully sweet, exceptionally gifted, and immensely talented friend, Jill Schoelen. "Thank you, Jill, for contributing all your extraordinary talents and professional touches to this project – you've been a real partner all along the way. You are so busy with the musical production project, yet you took time and devoted yourself to assisting me with the directing, the production and the videos I needed to make my dream a reality. I appreciate you deeply and you're my friend for life." 🙏

I thank Robert Schueller from Melissa's Produce for being my partner and sponsor on this journey, generously supplying me with all the gorgeous produce for the recipes, and for providing a wonderful media launch to premier this book. "Robert, I'm happy and grateful to be part of Melissa's Produce story." 🙏

A big thank you to Norik Shahbandarian from the Village French Bakery in Glendale for being my sponsor for all the beautiful bread he provided.   "Thanks, Norik – delicious breads!" 🙏

A most talented photographer extraordinaire that I ever met is Delaram Pourábdi. "I am so fortunate, Delaram, for you taking on this project. I thank you from the bottom of my heart for infusing your magical energy and vision into each and every photo, making the food so mouthwatering delicious looking, you want to eat it right off the page!" 🙏

I thank my dear friend of 36 years, Ramona Yoh, for being my set decorator and food stylist. "Ramona, you have also been an inspiration to me with your creativity, styling and your friendship. I knew that when you stepped in to by my stylist that your exquisite contribution would turn out great." 🙏

Thank you to my assistant Danielle Hershman. "Danielle, I always appreciate how you go above and beyond what is expected." 🙏

I want to especially thank Olivia Isabella Lee for being our video editor who definitely went above and beyond to capture the essence of the energy in all of the footage that we shot. "You have a great career ahead of you, Olivia, and I am forever grateful you were sent my way." 🙏

I thank my other assistant, Emily Stoltzman, for being such a devoted, conscientious assistant intern and fabulous make-up artist. "Emily, you just amaze me. You bring such a lighthearted, professional touch to everything you do as part of the support team." 🙏

Dillon Neal, Dante Marinelli and Kassi Cooper made up a great team for all the technical production and social media aspects for this book. Thank you. 🙏

Heather Priamos, from Secret Garden Hair and Make-up Studio was a master at doing my hair and make-up. "Thank you, Heather, I appreciate you so much." 🙏

My sister-in-law, Lani Silver, generously offered her lovely backyard for all the lifestyle shots. It was truly the perfect place to take photos of the family. "A gracious thank you, Lani, for being such a wonderful part of this project." 🙏

I want to acknowledge the Paper House Publishing Company team for approaching this project with the greatest of regard. "Thank you, Mo and Tiffany, for making the publishing process so easy and efficient. I appreciate all the care and love you devoted to this book." 🙏

Sometimes people step into your life and stay for the long haul no matter what. "I'm talking about you, Sam Herr, my beautiful friend for life who always steps up when something is needed of you. As the Chief Food Preparer, you helped with the cooking for this book. Thank you for providing your preparation touches with such nurturing kindness, and for always managing to find the humor in life." 🙏

Foreword

Being mindful of the way in which we live our lives is ultimately our responsibility. That's why I love this book. Shelley Whizin, the author of "What Do You Bring to the Table?" dives into ways of being mindful, using food as the impetus for change. Being a nutrition and exercise mentor/coach myself, I know that what Shelley brings to the table can inspire and change people's lives as well as their perspectives. It inspires an engagement to better the quality of each one's life cycle. This book has the ability to catalyze advancement through inner work and I believe this book is the utmost way the universe will bring her voice to those around the world who need to hear it the most. The concepts, life lessons, meditations and family recipes you will find in this book are a culmination of over three decades of experience. Shelley has helped countless individuals from all walks of life shift un-serving thoughts to ones that serve through a combination of two interesting methodologies she calls, "Soul Diving™", and "Instinct Cooking".

Perhaps you've entered the kitchen once or twice half "asleep" – no worries. Shelley will wake you up to experience living life to the fullest, and share with you how to be focused mindfully, especially when nourishing your family and friends through food. This book is for you, me, and all of us. You care enough to take responsibility for what you bring to the table of your life.

This is not a typical cookbook. It's a book that focuses more on using food as a way "in" to be attentive about what we, as human beings, bring to the table of life, not just what we "get." Indulging in cooking up the simple recipes using wholesome food nurtures the body as well as the soul, and will result in lifting the readers' spirits and "healing" hearts.

Shelley Whizin is a unique, one-of-a-kind human being that I have the privilege of calling my "friend for life". This is a term she has coined that creates an intimate friendship where both people agree to bring his/her authenticity and genuine care into the relationship. Shelley's spirit and friendship have become etched in the essence of my soul. Shelley is of pure heart and lives what she teaches, bringing love into everything she does with honor, dignity, and regard. She also brings a zest for life and an authenticity that touches people and engages them. She is truly dedicated to the knowledge of human betterment. When Shelley speaks, people stop and listen. There are times I cannot believe God created a person so versatile and open in heart and mind.

Her approach to cooking uses whole ingredients that most people already have in their fridge and pantry with simple steps and preparations that are easy to follow. The fun part, Shelley suggests, is using your instincts to add to the recipes to make them your own.

When you read this book, do take the time to do her *Happy Mindful Meditations*. They are designed to help you dive into your deepest self, discovering new and exciting "essences" of yourself, those special ingredients that come to the surface, to finally bring those essences of you to the table of your own life in the most supportive ways.

As Shelley always says as her own life's signature, "It's your life. Enjoy the journey. And remember to bring love into everything you do."

-Sima Cohen
@Simacohenofficial

Preface

Realization

"If more of us valued food and cheer and song above hoarded gold,
it would be a merrier world."

-J.R.R. Tolkien

Being the oldest girl of five siblings, I grew up learning the basic skills of homemaking at a very early age. My older brother wasn't expected to "do" much of anything in the house, so all the household responsibility fell on my little shoulders. I was four when my first sister was born. Two years later, another brother came along, then four years later, my baby sister. I was 9½ when she was born. Both my parents worked, so I became the "little mother," cooking for seven, starting at age 8, and making sure the house was meticulously clean, including making everyone's beds, before my mother would get home from work.

I would love to tell you that our home was a place of solace, but it was not. I had all the responsibility with no authority. That does not make for a great recipe, but I made the best of what I had, and fell in love with cooking along the way, and in spite of my responsibilities, I took great pride in feeding the family. That pride has carried over to today, and I have to admit, most of whatever I make turns out pretty yummy delicious. I still cook enough for the whole neighborhood, even if I am cooking for myself. I simply divide whatever is left into containers and give it away to others. I love to share my food. It's my way of sharing love.

I decided to write this book to address one of the greatest lessons I have ever learned about living, and that is, *"What we bring to the table of life is more important than focusing on what we get from life,"* which is the basis for this "who-you-are-while-you-are-cooking" cookbook for life. It's about taking a Deep Dive to capture the unique essences that you bring to life. the Deep Dive exploration may lead to identifying what thoughts/patterns may be getting in the way of bringing love into everything you do, including cooking in the kitchen.

We all have stories of our childhood growing up. Some memories are endearing, and some memories are not so wonderful. We learn how to be and how not to be, modeled after our parents. Often, we need to unlearn what our conditioned mind has learned, because the thoughts and beliefs we carry may be based on faulty belief systems. Once we identify these thoughts and beliefs, we are able to see a different way of thinking, no longer stay victims of our past, take responsibility for our part, choose healthier thoughts, and ultimately change our lives for the better, to live happier, more joyful lives.

So, how do we get from there to here? How do we live a full and wonderful life, feeling blessed with a sense of well-being and enjoy ourselves along the way? We Re-*Mind* ourselves to focus on what's really important in the life we want to live, asking ourselves questions like, "What kind of human being do I want to be?" "How can I live the best version of myself today?" "What can I bring to the table of life?" Then, we get to incorporate those ingredients into our lives and share the essences of who we are with the world in which we live.

I have also been fascinated with the human/spiritual relationship, studying the human/spiritual dynamic my entire life through a myriad of life experiences. My fascination with spirituality has taken me down the road of studying with great spiritual masters in America, Peru, Ecuador, India, England, Australia, Canada, and Mexico. My fascination with how the human body works led me to studying yoga, neural linguistic reprogramming, meditation, neuroscience, quantum physics and epigenetics, among other human studies. One of my favorite statements that Dr. Joe Dispenza, a chiropractor and neuroscientist, says is "science is the contemporary language of spirituality". It helps me to understand how we manifest thought into form and how our thoughts affect our bodies and the lives we live. It is not rocket science. It's just common sense.

I am one of those proverbial students of life, forever learning something new, eager to apply what I learn, and having the great privilege of teaching what I learn to others, so they too can live a more joyful, meaningful and fulfilled life with a sense of well-being.

BEing human, we all have many things in common. One of them is the need to feed the body, mind, and spirit with sustenance. We can do that by simply being conscious of breathing, eating, thinking, feeling and doing.

BEing satiated and fulfilled depends on the thoughts we think, the beliefs we hold true, and the attitude we carry in whatever we do.

BEing a foodie my whole life, and enjoying the process of cooking as a form of meditation, it occurred to me that talking about what you bring to the table of life is the perfect topic to approach in this book, by using food and cooking as analogies to address the quality of life you want to live.

My deep passion for studying human spirituality led me to establish The Soul Diving Institute. Thus, BEing a Soul Diving master guide, teacher, trainer, and life coach, my workshops often include food I've made from items and ingredients brought by each participant. Now I'm very excited about sharing some *new* ingredients with you that you can add to your life's kitchen, that will hopefully fill up your pantry, as well as your soul, with a variety of ingredients to select from, to excite your taste buds, and spice up your life in an unrefined, natural way, whipping your thoughts into a form that is helpful and delightful.

I have learned that when we stop focusing on what we "get" from life, and spend more time focusing on the energy of what we "bring" to life, our lives change for the better. We become in alignment with our higher/truer selves and the Universe conspires to give us a life of unexpected surprises. Darryl Anka once said, *"Energy is everything and that's all there is to it. Match the frequency of the reality you want, and you cannot help but get that reality. It can be no other way. This is not philosophy. This is physics."* If everything is energy, then, it is up to us to be mindful of the energy we bring to the Table of Life through our thoughts, our words, our actions, and through the food we make for ourselves and others.

Who knew that we would be living through one of the most challenging times in history, the Covid-19 Pandemic? Families are home, secluded from their "normal" activities. Parents are working from home, children are learning from home. Everyone is at home together, facing feelings that can be stressful, even when making food. It's important to know that you can be in charge of your own inner world, your mind, your thoughts, your heart and the way you nourish your body, regardless of what is going on around you.

Preparing yourself and practicing in a way that's loving and kind will soak into your everyday life in a way that releases your natural sense of well-being, permeating your inner sanctuary, leaving a sweet, refreshing after taste in your mouth, while deepening and adding a richness to your life.

Throughout this book, you will read about the importance of focusing on healthy thoughts to better navigate your human experiences with a sense of ease and grace. The goal is to sustain that mouthwatering sense of inner peace, regardless of outside circumstances.

When you live mindfully, with love from your heart, you are more apt to feel connected to the energy that exists in all the Universe. Recognizing that you are a one-of-a-kind unique ingredient in the vast quantum soup of infinite possibilities, you will bring and express your own unique essences.

When you are in alignment with your heart, your mind, and your soul, you enrich and deepen the quality of your life, strengthening your relationships, starting with the most important one you have with yourself. Then, from this loving place, you are able to play with your instincts, making the most out of everything you do in your life, including the approach you use in the food you select, prepare, and serve. Do you make food with love? Do you wash dishes with joy? What essences do you choose to add into the recipe of your life?

Introduction

"A recipe has no soul, you, as the cook, must bring soul to the recipe."

-Thomas Keller, American Chef

This book is a *'who-you-are-while-you-are-cooking'* cookbook. It's very much what Thomas Keller said about the soul you bring to the recipe that you make and the life that you live. It's about you, family, food, and the quality of life you live. It's about taking a gentle deep Soul Diving™ journey into re-acquainting yourself with your own instincts, acknowledging your own abilities and desires. It's about exploring and discovering your own unique essences that you bring to the Table of Life. It's about how you feel when preparing a simply great meal before, during and after you have eaten it, savoring each morsel. It's about being happy and mindful when you are cooking.

Sometimes we have thoughts we haven't consciously visited in quite some time, those thoughts and beliefs that have been running our lives without even being aware of them anymore, like boiling water. The water just boils and when we are not aware, we forget the water is boiling, the water evaporates, and the bottom of the pot burns. Similarly, when we are not aware of what is boiling within us, the body goes on automatic, reacting to the thoughts and beliefs we believe are true, and the thoughts get "burned" in, not even taking into consideration that they may perhaps be based on a faulty belief system. This faulty belief system often keeps people from really feeling happiness and joy in their everyday living, and yet not fully knowing all the reasons this is so.

When we become conscious of what WE bring to the table of our lives, we get to take responsibility for changing our present and our future. When we notice our thoughts, our beliefs, our words, our tone, and our behavior, we discover that many of our thoughts need to be dusted off, cleaned, boiled, steamed, roasted, baked, flambeed or even blowtorched.

"Bring Love into Everything You Do" is my life's motto that I choose to live by every day. It is the grounding energy force in my life that brings a sense of well-being for me through everything the word "love" stands for: kindness, forgiveness, compassion, patience, understanding… all held with honor, dignity, and regard. I am so grateful that this unconditional "Love" is the yummy delicious essence I get to bring to the Table of my life. I hope it spreads your way.

I have included several of my favorite recipes throughout the book for two reasons: they are simply delicious, and I think you'll love their simplicity and taste, and, they will serve as the medium to practice being mindful while you are cooking. Some are family recipes that I make with my grandchildren, daughter and sister. Some are made-up recipes that I call, "Instinct Cooking recipes," where I may select 5 or 6 different recipes and pick out the ingredients that call out to me. I hope you make them with unrelenting desire.

You will see a formula for bringing your deep-dived essences to the Table of Life. You will find some thought-provoking quotes, some stories and anecdotes, as well as some ingredients to consider either adding or taking away to make your life even more yummy delicious.

There are ***Happy Mindful Meditations*** guiding you into self-awareness to discover the beautiful essences you have to bring. You will be gently guided on a brief *Soul Diving*™ journey that is savory, sensory, and inspirational, leading to the discovery of your own special essences. Each and every one has their unique blend. The secret is in the "bringing."

Feel free to indulge in the gentle guidance offered as preparations to cooking with the ***Happy Mindful Meditations.*** They're meant to stimulate self-reflection as you are in moments prior to preparing a meal. Feel free to write what you experienced in the spaces provided in the book. This offers a peaceful space for you to note your deeper understandings and connection with your true essences. You will also find ***Going Inward*** questions to ponder after you savor what you've cooked, illuminating how the ***Happy Mindful Meditation*** affected your cooking experience.

You will hear me say that often we think it's about what we "get" from life, but it's really about what we *bring to life* that matters. It's about exploring and discovering what your special essences are, and have them blossom, using them to flavor your own everyday life, and the lives of family, friends, and of those whom you meet. It's filling your life with quality, "yummy delicious moments." Are you bringing self-worth or self-doubt? Are you acknowledging, validating, and praising yourself, or are you waiting for someone to give you approval, so you feel better? Are you an authentic listener with a genuine interest, or are you so preoccupied with what you want to say that you don't listen fully? Do you show compassion or dismiss other people's "problems" thinking that your problems are more worthy? Do you demonstrate self-care for yourself first, so that you have the *energy* of love to bring to others?

Do you consciously bring a loving, joyous *energy* into what you cook and if not, what are you then eating? Are you eating frustrations, anger, and/or a myriad of feelings of dissatisfaction with life feelings? It might be time to stop feeding yourself toxic thoughts that eat away at your self-worth and replace them with abundant servings of the savory essences that live deeply within your true/higher self.

What would all of this look like in a recipe? Maybe it shows itself in a delicious Butternut Squash Ginger Carrot Instinct Soup, filled with hand-picked wholesome organic vegetables from Melissa's Produce, or maybe in a Silver Girls' Caramel Praline Cheesecake recipe passed down from one generation to another with ingredients you may not have thought to add.

Whatever form the recipe takes, it comes back to the same thing. When you take deeper stock of the true essences of who you are, you are able to serve in a variety of differently enhanced ways, dishing out a different flavor of your character. This can happen when you make the decision to remove those ingredients, sometimes words, that no longer serve you and add the ones, new beliefs/thoughts, that elevate and deepen the quality of your life and the lives of others. This is how you can let go of eating non-digestible slices of life that are ego-driven and replace them with abundant servings of the real savory essences from a heart-driven place that live deeply within your true self and want to be expressed.

We are all human, have human attributes, and can improve and deepen the quality of life just by allowing and accepting that we are human, that we make mistakes, that we are vulnerable, that we miss the boat sometimes, and yes, we even hurt each other by the things that we say and the behavior we may, at times, exhibit. Forgiveness is a healing remedy for that, and we'll talk about that too.

As human beings, we each have emotions. Each one of us feels. Each one of us experiences feelings of anger, impatience, compassion, frustration, and other emotions that rob us of our well-being. Each one of us senses. Each one also experiences some form of love because of a generally held belief that we, and "All That Is/Universal Life Force," is also made of love, regardless of circumstances. Love, forgiveness, and kindness for the self, and others, support us in elevating our state of BEing and elevates the flavors each one of us brings to the table of life.

When you allow yourself to BE human, you release yourself of harsh self-judgment and judgment of others as well and are willing and open to transform your experiences through self-evolved, empowered, and heart-driven behavior. This also becomes what you bring to the table of life. The American poet, Edwin Markham said, "All that we bring into the lives of others, comes back into our own."

Once you have followed the gentle guidance into your soul-dive, you may well get to experience and savor what it's like to direct your life from the inside out, and not the other way around. This is what I call the discovery of your Joy Factor. It's like a spiritual GPS system to get to the heart of the matter quickly, just as quick as deciding to remove/leave out those ingredients that no longer sing to your taste buds.

You will have the opportunity to measure the level of your own life's Joy Factor on the Joy Factor Scale, and you'll be reading more about this later in the book. Once you get an opportunity to see where you currently stand on this Scale, and where you want to BE, you can spend more time going towards the direction that you desire. This is akin to removing ingredients in a recipe that you don't particularly like and replacing them with ones that delight you.

Everything that is written in this book is not new. I'm sure you've heard many of the things and may have read similar concepts in different ways, many times. This book, however, expresses them in such a way so as to give you the Soul Diving experience to take-away and Re-*Mind* you of what you already know but may have forgotten. I truly hope that these Re-*Minders* help you navigate life with as much ease and grace as possible.

Here's a delicious recipe for life:

Thinking well = Eating well = Feeling well = BEing well = Well-being

Life is like a big pie with many slices. We spend time in different areas and sometimes we neglect areas that help keep us in balance and in alignment with our deeper/higher/true self. How much time we spend in any one area, reflects how big the slice is. When we neglect some of the most important parts of ourselves, it affects our health, our relationships, our careers, our creative expressions, our spirituality, our fun, our time, money, freedom, and our contribution to society, which really affects what we bring to the table.

This is why I chose to offer you **"Bite Size Re-*Minders* to Living a Yummy Delicious Life"** pulling five kernels of wisdom from each chapter as Re-*Minders* to live by. They are the sum total of precious "yummy delicious moments" that make up and elevate the quality of your everyday life, that you get to create, expand, and enhance. Savoring delicious moments allows each one of us to step into embracing happiness and joyful savoring of even the mundane things in life.

Throughout the book, you will notice that I state the basic amount of ingredients to add for each recipe. It is important that you start with a base, but what I want you to do is to feel out each recipe and add your own flair to what you are making by trusting your instincts. That's what cooking is all about: getting in touch with your own natural juices, and senses to "feel" the dish you are making and by adding your ingredients. When I make an Instinct Soup, I go to the market and "ask" which vegetables want to come home and be in my soup," and I hear them say, "I do, take me, I want to be in your soup", and they all come home with me and I create a soup. I call this "Instinct Cooking."

It is my greatest desire that you find your essences, that you bring out your ingredients in the most magnificent ways that shed light and radiate into the world. I do hope you enjoy reading this book as well as taking this special Soul Diving™ journey in cooking some of my favorite recipes.

Chapter Previews

In Chapter 1, "**Preparation of Self, Getting into the Deep-Dive**", I introduce the concept of *Happy Mindful Meditations* that you will find in each chapter. Chapter 1 sets the mood for how to prepare yourself, emotionally, physically, mentally, and spiritually before and after you cook.

In Chapter 2, "**Energy: The Boundless Spirit**", we're going to explore how energy/spirit *is* everything, *is in* everything, and *is around* everything, further delving into the reasons for its importance.

In Chapter 3, "**Heart-Driven: Increasing the Joy Factor**", we are going to talk about why it is so important to come from the heart and trust your inner GPS guidance system.

In Chapter 4, "**Relationships: Family & Friends**", we will dive into the importance of creating the healthiest relationships, starting with the one you have with yourself.

In Chapter 5, "**Love, Love, Love,**", you will experience the beauty of bringing love into everything you do.

In Chapter 6, "**Creating Your Sanctuary**", you will discover how important it is to create your home/sanctuary that reflects and supports your inner sanctum.

In Chapter 7, "**Change Your Thoughts, Change Your Life**", you will learn how the body goes on "automatic", and becomes the mind and how to change your life.

In Chapter 8, "**Connecting: Sharing and Caring,**" we will discuss the significance of connecting with each other and yourself.

In Chapter 9, **"New Way of BEing"**, you will learn how to live with a new shift in your personality by shifting your thoughts.

In Chapter 10, **"Living Your legacy"**, you will explore what it takes to BE what you want to pass on to others.

In Chapter 11, **"Contributing to the World"**, we will explore how you make a difference in life and how to pay it forward.

In the **Conclusion** we will tie it all together like a beautiful tossed salad.

You will also notice a **Glossary of Shelley's Terms**, offering you definitions of words I may use throughout the book to contextualize their meanings.

This entire book is about being in alignment with your mind, heart, body and soul, which means allowing yourself to be present, being conscious of enjoying every experience you are having, including cooking in the kitchen, with as much ease and grace as possible.

Now it's time to Deep-Dive into yourself, discover your essences, bring them into everything you cook and share them with those who have also brought their essences to the table of food and life.

I sincerely hope you take away new ways of thinking about what you bring to the table of your life.

It's your life. Enjoy the journey. And remember to bring love into everything you do.

Chapter 1

Preparation of Self – Getting into the Deep-Dive

"Cooking is a holistic process of planning, preparing, dining and sharing food. I place food at the center of our humanity, as it nourishes not only our physical bodies but also our emotional and spiritual lives. Food is truly a cultural phenomenon that informs our traditions and our relationship with the earth. I genuinely believe that food connects us all."

-Eric Frank Ripert, French Chef, Author, and Television Personality

As humans, we've been given 5 senses to experience: sight, touch, smell, hearing and taste, all of which can be connected to food. When we make something delicious, it tantalizes our sense of taste. With a beautiful presentation, our eyes get a treat. When something we make smells good, it opens up our olfactory system and we get to take in the delicious whiff that fills our soul with delight. When we hear the sounds of food cooking, it satisfies our sense of hearing. There's nothing like hearing the crackling of crisping something up in a pan. And the texture of fresh produce excites our sense of touch. Every food has a different texture, smell, taste, look and sound. Pay attention to all of your senses when you are preparing, cooking and serving the food you have made with love.

Sometimes we have to prepare ourselves to get into a particular mindset to tackle an activity. We may not be "in the mood" for cooking, and we just want to rush through it to get it over with. Have you ever felt like that? We may be preoccupied with all the other things on the to-do list, resulting in not really being present when we are making food.

Maybe you had a "challenging" experience a couple of days prior that threw you off kilter, that shifted your energy, and you can't seem to shake it. You are still carrying around the negative emotions and go into the kitchen to make food with this energy tainting your potentially enjoyable experience.

Think of your body as a big pot and all the thoughts you think are the ingredients you put into the pot to make a big stew. As you know, being a cook, you need to stir the pot often enough to prevent the ingredients from sticking to the bottom. Sometimes our thoughts get stuck, and also need to be stirred up, so we can bring them to the surface and identify what needs to be removed with a big spatula.

Sometimes we need to stew in the juices of our own making and feel all the human emotions, and sometimes we even have to soak the pot overnight in order to remove what seemingly appears to be embedded in the bottom that it discolors the pot.

So, how do you get ready to Deep-Dive before even preparing to cook? You may want to adopt it as a good practice to always begin with a *Happy Mindful Meditation,* helping you pause long enough to shift from one experience to another. Find your sense of stillness before you begin creating the meal that you want to prepare for yourself, your family and/or your friends. It's about taking a -time out-, quieting the inner chatter, just for a moment or two, to get in touch with the essence of you, the joy of you, the love of you.

When you take the time for yourself, even for a brief moment, you are acknowledging the "in-between-space" (the NOW) that exists in life with a sense of regard. It's important not to dismiss this "in-between-space" as nothing. ALL the moments in your life are important, not just the ones that are next on your list of "to do's". It's the experience you are conscious of having right here and now in the space you occupy that is the most important moment to acknowledge. That's called BEing in the present.

Giving yourself a few moments to gather your energy to become conscious of what you are bringing into your own experience makes all the difference in the world. Are you savoring THIS moment? Do you genuinely enjoy what you are doing, whatever that may be or are you incessantly ruminating about thoughts you can't do anything about that bring you down (right now), keeping you in the past?

Just noticing what comes up, without judgment is a step in the right direction. Once you begin to detach from those thoughts and use your senses to be present, the chatter will quiet down to make space for the current moment.

These *Happy Mindful Meditations* are a gift for you. You deserve to take time for yourself. Give yourself permission and find a quiet place, even if you need to sequester yourself in a bathroom for one whole minute to close your eyes and get in touch with your sweet essence. You're worth it, because it truly does change the quality of your experience and will affect the lives of those around you. Consider the time you take like spiritually lassoing your scattered energy into one cohesive place.

When you no longer dismiss the joy that you feel in being present, you actually get to enjoy the experiences you are having. When you focus on being grateful for being alive, for the gift of BEing human, you are able to transform one emotion to another.

Before we continue, I would like to draw your attention to two ingredients that help you BE and STAY in the moment:

3

1. BEing aware of the "in-between-space" using your senses (where you are).

2. BEing aware of your breath, (keeping you where you are)

We're going on a Soul Diving™ journey into the world through food, into the world of your senses, into the world of thoughts and beliefs, and into the world of consciousness. Get ready to take a bite!

BEing in the In-Between - Space

Everything in life, including humans, is made up of mostly space. There is space between here and there. There is space between now and then. There is space between an inhale and an exhale, night and day, standing and sitting, going and coming, and there is space in between all the parts of our body. In fact, atoms are 99.99999% space[1] so honoring the "in between" space is a juicy ingredient to remember. When you create space consciously within you, your mind can expand and reach the outer limits of the Universe where anything is possible in the Land of Infinite Potential.

The space you occupy right now is really the only experience you are having, now, so being consumed with an experience you had in the past that brings you down, will only assure that you'll have the same experience in the future and robs you of the ability to BE present in this moment. Einstein said, "Insanity is doing the same thing over and over, expecting a different result."

---

[1] https://www.sciencealert.com/99-9999999-of-your-body-is-empty-space

Honor where you are. Look at where your feet are planted. Be conscious of who is the cook cooking the food, observe the energy you are bringing into your experience.

If you're still entertaining thoughts that are taking you down, be aware of them, pause and stop for just a moment, gather yourself, set a new intention of how you want to BE, and then begin to prepare your meal.   For example, instead of thinking everything is an upheaval, and being preoccupied with what you still have to do, shift your mindset to seeing the experience as something you "get to do", becoming in alignment with your heart. What's the point of doing something rushed without bringing yourself into the experience, being mindful or heartful?

Since everything is energy, you get to be the CEO (Chief Energy Officer) of your own experiences. After all, you are the one in charge of your energy, are you not?

BEing with Your Breath - Your Internal Stress Reducer

Breathing is something you do all day long that you don't usually have to think about. However, paying attention to your breath can be a powerful practice in the art of focusing, can immensely relieve stress, and calm the nervous system. Have you ever noticed how you breathe when you feel relaxed? The next time you are relaxed, take a moment to notice how your body feels.

Deep breathing is one of the best ways to lower stress in the body. This is because when you breathe deeply, it sends a message to your brain to calm down and relax. The brain then sends this message to your body.[2]

Breathing exercises can help you relax because they make your body feel as it

_____

[2] https://chopra.com/articles/breathing-for-life-the-mind-body-healing-benefits-of-pranayama

does when it is already relaxed.

As humans, we are all born with an inhale, and leave this world with an exhale. It's what we do with all the breaths in between that matter. We can cry over spilled milk and the burnt turkey we left in the oven too long, or we can just allow ourselves to BE human, knowing that we make mistakes, BE kind and gentle to ourselves, and remember to breathe as much as possible.

Breath = life. In Genesis 2.7, it was written: "*And God breathed life into the nostrils of man.*" That means we are breathing in our own spirit! I cannot emphasize enough the importance of being conscious of breathing. We cannot survive without our breath. Our breath is our own life force that animates us, that keeps us alive as walking, active, thinking, human BEings.

Breathing is one of the BEST remedies for stress, because when you consciously breathe, you are bringing in more oxygen to your cells and all of your organs and systems run better, more efficiently, with more energy, and you feel better too. What could be better than feeling better?

As children, we were told so many no's - and don'ts, that as adults, we forget how to breathe in our natural way. Ever watch a baby breathe? Its tummy goes up and down. When we are not aware of how we breathe, we cut off the lower portion of our bodies, where our crucial survival energy centers are, and we breathe from the chest up. How can we not feel stress or tension when we are always on fight or flight/ adrenaline producing stress mode?

When we breathe deeply into our diaphragm (belly breath), we bring that sweet and vibrant oxygen into our bodies, filling up our cells, lifting our spirits and feeling calm, just by focusing on the breath.

Bite Size Re-*Minders* to Living a Yummy Delicious Life

- I remember to prepare and be mindful before I cook to BE present.

- I remember to take time out and quiet the inner chatter to find my inner calm.

- I remember when I take time for myself, I am honoring myself.

- I remember to be conscious of my breath throughout the day.

- I remember I am the CEO (Chief Energy Officer) of my own life.

Happy Mindful Meditation #1
Breathing/Thinking Something Happy/Joyful

Every athlete prepares him/herself mentally, physically, emotionally, and spiritually before they do what they do. Every actor prepares for a scene, also getting their energy into a high state of BEing. An athlete may run to warm up his/her muscles. An actor may jump up and down or also run around to get his/herself in a high state of energy to be fully present.

We've talked about how the breath is one of the key factors in helping us to "get" present. We also know, without breath we would not be alive. Savoring our breath and BEing conscious of breathing is one of the quickest ways to BE present. We don't "have to" be conscious of breathing, because a higher force is breathing us. However, when we are not conscious of breathing "properly" and deeply, we cut the rest of our body off, robbing ourselves of the precious oxygen we need to thrive and feel great.

This first *Happy Mindful Meditation* helps you to get in touch with your breath, making all the difference in the world in how you feel and how you think. Adding something happy and joyful to contemplate elevates not only the thoughts you think, but the emotions you experience. When you think thoughts that are in alignment with your emotions, you feel the essence of well-being. I hope you enjoy your happy mindful moment.

- Find a quiet comfortable place, ensuring yourself that your time and space are regarded without interruption (if you have kids, do the best you can, or bring them into the experience… who knows? They might like a happy mindful moment too!)

- Sit comfortably and begin by being conscious of your breathing.

- Focus on your breath, inhaling and exhaling, all the way down into your belly, inflating your stomach as you inhale and pulling it in as you exhale.

- Notice how you take in air, and how you release air, breathing deeply.

- As you breathe in, count to 4, slowly, deliberately and consciously.

- As you exhale, also count to 4, easily and effortlessly, controlling your breathing in and out in a rhythmic pattern. This helps to calm your mind of chatter as you focus on your breathing. Feeling your body beginning to relax.

- Imagine your lungs enjoying this wonderful time where air is filling them up, replenishing them with calm rhythmic breathing.

- Now, think of something positive you did that made you happy, that made you feel joyful for hours and even days. It could be winning a prize in school, or getting married, or finally affording that week of vacation in an exotic place, whatever you deem that gave you that feeling of euphoria for some accomplishment you achieved. Whatever comes to mind. Let it permeate every cell of your being. Feel the goosebumps on your arms.

- Now that you have this in your mind, feel those moments all over again, really letting yourself get into them, and *Deep Dive* further to identify what was that essence that brought about your "win".

- Once you identify that essence, hang on to it in your mind, savor it anew in your heart, and repeat it to yourself. And feel it, if you won something and you got excited, let yourself feel it right here right now.

- Then, when you are ready, gently open your eyes, take a moment and write down this particular essence.

Going Inward Before the Meal

Take a moment to feel your essence, connect with it, and own it. What came up for you? Was it "resilient", "confident", "hard worker", "calm person"? Was it "feeling loved"? Whatever words or phrases that come up from your *Deep Dive* is an essence of you that you bring into your cooking and to the Table of Life. You have now prepared yourself to begin cooking and bringing your essence into what you will make and what you will bring to the Table of Life.

_____

_____

_____

_____

Butternut Squash Ginger Carrot Instinct Soup

This soup is part of my "Instinct Soup" Collection. I picked out different ingredients from 5 different recipes that were calling to me and made this one up. Feel free to do the same. Add your favorite ingredients that call to you! Remember these are basic ingredients, so if something else comes to you, or you want to leave something out, trust yourself and put it in or take it out. Life is an experiment anyway. Imagine you are making the BEST Butternut Ginger Carrot Soup EVER and FEEL what that feels like. You can use strictly vegetarian ingredients for this one! Make it a fun experience/experiment. Trust what you want! ENJOY!

Serves 6
Prep time: 25 minutes
Cook time: 40 minutes
Total time: 1h 5m

Ingredients

2 Tbs butter, room temperature
2 Tbs extra-virgin olive oil
1 Lg onion or 2 med onions, chopped
3 Tbs minced garlic
1 thumb of ginger, peeled, grated, or chopped
2 tsp ginger paste
¼ tsp cinnamon
½ tsp mild yellow curry powder
½ tsp turmeric
2 lb. butternut squash, chopped
1 med sweet potato, peeled & chopped
3 carrots, peeled & chopped
2 apples cubed into 1-inch pieces
1 32-oz organic chicken or vegetable stock
3 Tbs Better than Bouillon chicken or vegetable
¼ cup maple syrup
½ cup squeezed orange juice
1 tsp salt
Pinch of pepper
¼ cup roasted pumpkin seeds as garnish
Cilantro as garnish on the top

Method

Chop up all of your ingredients first, especially the onion and ginger.

In a large soup pot, warm 2 tablespoons olive oil and room temperature butter over medium heat until simmering.

Add the chopped onion, minced garlic, ginger, cinnamon, curry, turmeric and salt. Cook, stirring often until the onion is softened and starting to turn golden on the edges (about 3-4 minutes) and you can smell the fragrance. Stir occasionally, scraping the bottom of the pot. Don't forget to SMELL everything cooking, that's half the fun!

Add the squash, carrots, potatoes, and apples to the pot.

Stir all of the vegetables and let cook for about 10 minutes.

Add organic chicken or veggie stock, making sure all the vegetables are covered. Bring just to a boil, then turn the burner down to medium.

Add the maple syrup, squeezed orange and reduce the heat to low.

Cover pot, and simmer 25 minutes, or until all vegetables are tender.

Transfer half (or however much your instincts tell you) of the soup to a blender, leaving some of the vegetable pieces in the pot. Blend until smooth. Make sure you have the lid fastened on tightly with a little air to release the steam.

Return the blended mixture to the pot and mix any remaining stock to attain desired desired taste and consistency.

Season with salt and pepper and serve.

Add a sprig of cilantro for a garnish on the top and a few pumpkin seeds.

Garlic Bread Grilled Cheese Sandwiches

I was babysitting my grandkids one night and thought to myself it would be a great idea to make a twist on a regular grilled cheese sandwich, so I added a garlic butter spread. It turned out sooooo good. I hope you enjoy.

Serves 4
Prep time: 15 minutes
Cook time: 10 minutes
Total time: 25 minutes

Ingredients

8 slices Sourdough Wheat Bread
8 slices of cheddar cheese
1 cup of butter at room temperature
¼ cup extra virgin olive oil
1 tsp garlic powder
3 tsp fresh minced garlic
¼ tsp salt
¼ tsp Everything but the Bagel Seasoning
Pinch of finely chopped parsley or basil

Suggestion: You can also serve this with Zoe's Fun Fruity Nutty Salad in Chapter 11. Use the recipes for mixing and matching your tastes.

Method

In a mixing bowl, put the soft butter, olive oil, garlic powder, fresh minced garlic, salt, and Everything but the Bagel Seasoning. Mix well. Taste to see if it's garlicy enough. (I can never have enough garlic)

Spread the garlic butter mixture on one side of 8 slices of the bread.

Heat a sauté pan to medium high, place one slice in the pan, buttered side down.

Place one (or two) slice(s) of cheese on the top of the bread in the pan and cover it with the top of the sandwich (other buttered side up).

Heat until golden brown, then with a spatula, turn the sandwich upside down and cook the other side until golden brown. The cheese will be melted.

Remove from pan, place on plate. I like to cut it into quarters diagonally for the fun of it.

Going Inward After the Meal

Now that you have finished cooking, get yourself a journal or a pad, and write down how the Deep-Dive into the discovery of your essence impacted your cooking experience. Did the memory you thought about that brought up feelings of confidence and a sense of achievement alter the way you cooked? This model will be used throughout the book, doing a Happy Mindful Meditation before you cook, reflecting on the essence you are bringing into the experience of cooking, and then taking a few moments after the meal to reflect on the whole experience. Did you enjoy the experience? Did it help you to become more present and aware? What was the result for you? Were there any responses from your family and friends?

Self-Reflections/Notes

Chapter 2

Energy: The Boundless Spirit

"If you eat fresh foods that have a living energy,
the food returns that living energy."

-Simon Brown

Have you ever imagined the "end" of the Universe? It's so vast that we can't possibly visualize its infiniteness. All living things are part of this living energy that exists in the boundless spirit of the Universe. It cannot be any other way, because we are all made up of the same energy (particles and waves) that exist everywhere in space. The thoughts we think, the beliefs we hold, and the foods we eat impact the energy within us and around us.

Since energy exists in, throughout, and around everything, it makes sense then fresh foods containing this living energy would affect the way we feel when we eat the food. It is the same with the attitude and thoughts we carry wherever we are, even into the kitchen. Since we too are living energy, whatever energy we are carrying, based on the thoughts we are thinking exudes that energy out.

The energy we carry has an impact on the "way" in which we approach everything we do, even in making food. The point being, when you are cooking, wouldn't you want to enjoy the process of cooking, while you are cooking, and let yourself experience the delight in creating inventive, delicious and scrumptious foods?

Energy is a big topic. I could write an entire book, just on energy alone, but for the purposes of this book, I'm going to touch on a few key points about how energy affects us from a scientific and a spiritual perspective, even while cooking.

Energy converts from one form to another. That is a scientific fact. No matter what we do, we cannot destroy energy. This is based on one of my favorite laws of Thermodynamics, stating that "energy can be changed from one form to another, but it cannot be created or destroyed".[3] I love that Law! Energy just "IS". Energy is eternal, and changing form is the fun part.

We can **heat** something up on the stove and transform it from one form to another. When we cook rice, for example, we boil the water, put the hard, dry rice kernels into that pot of boiling water, and within a short period of time, the rice changes form, from being hard and inedible to becoming soft and appetizing. The same is true when we **freeze** something in the freezer, like water for example, it changes form by freezing the liquid into what appears to be "solid" ice cubes. When we take the ice cubes out, they eventually melt with time, returning to their original form, going back to being a liquid. Voila! Magic! Transforming from one form to another!

We can apply this same law to the thoughts we think. Sometimes we need to heat up and get "disturbed" in order for us to change a thought from one form to another. Change doesn't usually happen when we are complacent.

Being disturbed is not necessarily a "bad" thing. The word connotes something being shaken up but think about it this way: When a grain of sand enters

[3] https://courses.lumenlearning.com/boundless-chemistry/chapter/the-laws-of-thermodynamics/

an oyster shell, the oyster gets "disturbed" and "irritated". What does it do? It secretes a fluid that covers the grain of sand and with time, turns it into a beautiful pearl. There are pearls of wisdom within each and every one of us that come out when we are disturbed, when we stir the pot, so to speak, allowing the sediments on the bottom to come to the surface, I believe, is all in the name of healing. It doesn't always feel like it, taste like it, sound like it or look like it, but a healing nonetheless is going on for our soul's journey.

Here's another way to look at it. When we are conscious as an "observer", we can actually change a stress-inducing thought into a thought of well-being, thus "disturbing" the current neural pathway[2] circuit, carrying the negative thought. Liken this to an electrical circuit, giving it a new directive that rewires the neurons[3] and changes the form into a new thought. Phew! Research shows that "neurons that wire together fire together".[4] We actually go through a process of "unlearning" certain conditioning, and "rewiring" neural pathways, so that we can think different thoughts. We'll talk more about this in Chapter 7, **"Change Your Thoughts, Change your Life".** So, how do you rewire these neurons to better thinking/feeling thoughts?

One way to rewire your brain is to be mindful and aware of the thoughts you carry, which help you to stay present. It's being an "observer" of your own thinking, slightly detaching and not taking anything personally. If you are stressed out before making a meal, using any of the *Happy Mindful Meditations* will help you to stay aware of your thoughts, so you can consciously shift your thinking, allowing yourself to be fully present and have a more pleasant experience while you are cooking. That makes sense, right?

---

[4] https://themindisthemap.com/neurons-that-fire-together-wire-together/

Humans don't come with instruction manuals. We need to figure everything out as we go along. Sometimes we make the "outside" world more important than our internal existence. Any opportunity to go inside, pause and explore our inner world helps us to grow into healthier, kinder, more aware human beings, and when you are more aware and enter the kitchen, about to prepare a meal, you are more apt to feel good and be happy before you cook, wouldn't you agree?

Based on the premise that we are spiritual BEings having a human experience, it's the human part that presents the bumpy ride. It's up to us to determine how we navigate that journey. Talking about the basics of energy is important, because it is what makes us who we are.

I use the word "energy" intertwined with the word "spirit" because I believe that spirit = energy. It's what animates us. It's what breathes us. It's what digests our food and helps us to cleanse our bodies. It's energy that runs through our veins. It's what we put into our cooking. It's how we express ourselves. Without energy/spirit, there would be no "us" in this human form.

Science has evolved to such a state that, as Dr. Joe Dispenza says, it has become the contemporary language for spirituality. Invisible energy can be explained scientifically, and there is so much research to prove that the energy of thoughts directly affects the quality of life we live. If you know complainers, their lives usually provide great evidence to continue believing their beliefs. My contention is if the energy we use can make us stressed out and sick, then that same energy can make us feel calm and well, just switching the focus. Whatever we focus our energy on expands. What would you prefer to focus on in your life?

Here's the dilemma. The study of anthropology, science, sociology, biology and other sciences show that all animals (including humans) are wired to be on alert for impending danger.[5] It was normal to fear predators in the caveman days, because it was highly likely that a hungry wild animal would be lurking around the bend. Humans were on high alert, and rightfully so, most of the time! Our reptilian brains would signal "DANGER AHEAD" and would warn us to either run like the dickens or fight (fight or flight response when a physiological reaction that occurs in response to a perceived harmful event, attack or threat to our survival.)

In this day and age, we don't have the same wild animals prowling the streets, but our minds don't know the difference between a fear that is "real" or a fear that is "made up", (*can you believe that*), and our body responds to the fear imposed, real or not. The reptilian part of our brain is there to protect us, no question about that, and our neocortex part of our brain allows us to think and override the survival wiring.

When we are cooking, and if we're carrying fearful, negative, angry, and unresolved thoughts, the energy of those thoughts goes into whatever we are doing and even enters into the food we are making. It's up to us to clear our minds of any negativity so we infuse the food with LOVE. Filling the heart with gratitude helps us to center, ground and focus on something that makes us feel better. So, how do we do that?

Remember I said it takes practice? Here is another opportunity to practice staying aware, awake and conscious of your thoughts, your actions and your demeanor/temperament. Use this *Happy Mindful Meditation* to go inside and gently quiet all the hum that goes on in that beautiful brain of yours. I don't suggest exercises I don't do myself, and I know I feel better when I take those special, precious moments for me. When you take the time for you, you feel better. It's as

---

[5] Definition of reptilian brain

simple as that. Try it on for size, like you're going shopping, to see how it feels. My bet is that you WILL feel better.

Bite Size Re-*Minders* to Living a Yummy Delicious Life

- I remember that energy can be changed from one form to another, but never destroyed.
- I remember that my energy is the same energy that makes up the particles and waves in the boundless Universe.
- I remember that my thoughts are also made up of the same living energy as the foods we eat and impact the way in which we live.
- I remember that I am able to transform my thoughts from one form to another, by changing my perspective.
- I remember that being "disturbed" or "heated" up is a healthy kind of stress that is an important ingredient to my growth as a human being.

Happy Mindful Meditation #2
Cup of Tea Sensations/Sitting with Stillness

Giving yourself permission to relax is a HUGE deal! When you allow yourself to pause, breathe and be aware of the in-between-space, you have given yourself a gift of time out to relax and melt into a deep state of rejuvenation, relaxation and inspiration. All of this can happen in moments.

When there's nowhere else to go, and nothing else to do in the moments you give yourself, there is a sense of freedom, that your life is your own, that you call the shots, and that you create the inner calm center. Remembering that you are the CEO (Chief Energy Officer) of your own energy, you remind yourself that you have officially taken charge. Good for you! You're worth it.

This *Happy Mindful Meditation* is letting you have a relationship with the stillness of yourself through a cup of tea, I hope you enjoy your mindful moment.

- Pick your favorite tea and prepare it. Use your sense of smell to take in the aromatic fragrance of the tea you chose and the warmth emanating from the cup as your senses begin to awaken.

- Find a quiet comfortable place, ensuring yourself that your time and space are regarded without interruption.

- Quietly drink your beautiful cup of tea and focus on all the flavors and sensations it brings you in your mouth.

- Let your thoughts go, feeling a sense of quiet/stillness even for a few seconds.

- Savor those seconds as precious gifts you are giving yourself.

- Stay with that focus until you discover an essence that your stillness has brought you as you enjoy a cup of tea.

Going Inward Before the Meal

See? It's simple and it doesn't take longer than a moment or two. In fact, as you practice this, the feeling of stillness can happen in a nanosecond. We're just starting with a moment or two. It's fun to discover an essence of yourself. There are many essences brewing inside of you that are ready to come out. You can identify one essence at a time, or maybe several came to the surface. Keep alive in your mind what essence that came up for you. You are now ready to bring the energy of that essence to your cooking and to the Table of Life.

_____

_____

_____

_____

Mike's Mighty Mediterranean Chopped Salad

My son in law, Mike, was a professional baseball player, and the whole family is very sports oriented and health conscious, so here's a little different twist on one of his very favorite salads I learned to make while living in Israel years ago. We call it, an "Israeli" salad, and it's also called an "Arabic" salad, and it all comes from the Mediterranean/Middle East, so whatever name you call it, it's good. By adding super seeds, like chia seeds and hemp seeds, it not only adds a fun crunch factor, it's super nutritious, a great source of omega 3's and minerals like magnesium and zinc. 6 ! Mike loves it! Use your instincts to get the salad just the way you like it. Remember these are the base ingredients. Feel free to add what inspires you. Whatever you add will taste great! ENJOY!

Serves 4-6

Prep time: 20 minutes

Ingredients

10 Persian cucumbers

4 Lg tomatoes or 2 pks cherry tomatoes

2 heads Romaine lettuce

½ bunch organic cilantro

¼ cup slivered toasted almonds

1 Tbs sesame seeds,

1 Tbs hemp seeds

1 Tbs chia seeds

½ tsp Everything but the Bagel seasoning

¼ tsp salt

¼ tsp garlic powder

Pinch of pepper

3 Tbs extra virgin olive oil

3 lemons

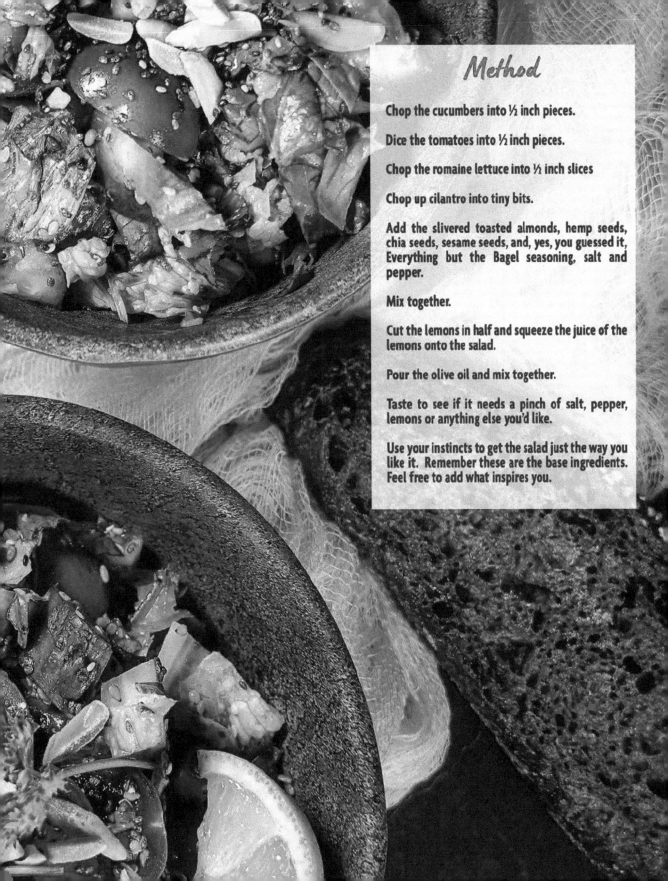

Method

Chop the cucumbers into ½ inch pieces.

Dice the tomatoes into ½ inch pieces.

Chop the romaine lettuce into ½ inch slices

Chop up cilantro into tiny bits.

Add the slivered toasted almonds, hemp seeds, chia seeds, sesame seeds, and, yes, you guessed it, Everything but the Bagel seasoning, salt and pepper.

Mix together.

Cut the lemons in half and squeeze the juice of the lemons onto the salad.

Pour the olive oil and mix together.

Taste to see if it needs a pinch of salt, pepper, lemons or anything else you'd like.

Use your instincts to get the salad just the way you like it. Remember these are the base ingredients. Feel free to add what inspires you.

Going Inward After Eating the Meal

Sitting in stillness with a cup of tea could have definitely altered the way in which you entered the kitchen. Did you allow yourself to enjoy your cup of tea, even for those brief moments? How was your experience? How did the Deep-Dive into the discovery of your essence affect your cooking? Were you aware than anything changed at all? Take a moment and write down what came up, and your experience of cooking changed. Were there any responses from your family and friends?

Self-Reflections/Notes

Chapter 3
Heart-Driven: The Joy Factor

"Only the pure of heart can make a good soup."

-Ludwig van Beethoven

Beethoven somehow understood the importance of connecting music and appreciating soup-making from a pure heart. Both involve creativity from the heart. He lived to create the most magnificent symphonies, even though he became deaf in his later life. His deafness didn't stop him from hearing with his "inner" ear and seeing with his "inner" eyes from the heart.

Soups, stews and sauces always taste better the next day. The settling of the mixture somehow saturates the flavors even more. When we are heart-driven, we exude and bring out those yummy delicious flavors in ourselves reflected in a wide variety of feelings emanating from pure love. Being consciously heart-driven re-awakens the very essences that help us steep in a sense of joy, kindness, honor and regard, among other essences that make up for a joyful, happy life.

There is nothing like waking up in the morning and "still" feeling a sense of well-being and calm in your heart from the day before. Feelings abound with a sense of love and possibilities. Void of this awareness in our life would make us almost oblivious that we might have been living a less than desirable way of living.

It can take time to calibrate the right formula, but there's one thing for sure, when we come from love and are heart-driven, we are rewiring our brains into experiencing a heart/mind coherence, and over time, this pattern becomes the "new norm". Once we get the recipe right, and we follow it from the heart, we are able to sustain joy creating a new neural pathway that we have nurtured over time, one that is healthy and conducive for right-minded-thinking and heart-minded-feeling. This too takes practice. Over time, we are able to rewire and re-fire the neurons in our brain, setting a new default button, and joy is on the way of BEing a natural part of living.

In 1988 I gave a workshop to a group of Jewish educators called, "What About You?" (WAY), which explores the ways in which individuals who constantly are in service to others can learn how to nurture themselves. In attendance were leaders in the Jewish communities from all over the country who were on the "front lines", working directly with families, often trading their own family time for the sake of the larger community. This is one example of community leaders who bring the essences of their heart-driven self to the Table of Life. At that time, I wondered, "Who nurtures them?" Thus, the "What About You" (WAY) workshop was born, because I wanted to bring something to them that would be nurturing.

WAY is continuously relevant as every giving person can use these tools offered with guided ways and means to implement nurturing our spiritual self in a conscientiously loving way that energizes us to continue giving and being of service, especially in our own families.

WAY includes learning various breathing techniques based on how I learned to teach yoga. It also involves learning some stretches to maintain flexibility in body, mind and heart.

One of the exercises I created, was called the Joy Factor Scale where I asked the class to stand on an invisible scale from 1 to 10, based on where they usually hover in their daily lives most of the time. One wall of the classroom represented ultimate JOY at a 10, and the other wall represented being miserable/dissatisfied/discontent at a 1. Astonishingly, the majority of the participants in the class stood between a 3 and a 4! That meant that *most* of the time they lived their lives not even half-way to their optimum Joy Factor. You can measure your own Joy Factor in life by looking at the Joy Factor Scale below.

Increasing the Joy Factor in our own life involves taking a bit of time out to get still, to breathe, to meditate, do yoga, dance, listen to music, sing, laugh and other playful methods of nurturing ourselves that speak directly to you. The aim is to sustain a sense of joy, not just "visit" it.

When we use a slow cooker that we set on automatic, we don't think about what "it's" doing, because it will turn off when it's "done", and it is definitely a positive experience. However, when we live our lives in a similar manner on automatic, we may not even be conscious nor realize that we are living less than a wonderful life. We may think it's just "normal' to live that way. Maybe because we're "used to it", it's "familiar" and that's what we saw being modeled by our parents growing up – I know I did.

For so many years I thought I would be sad and depressed my whole life, that it was genetic and "normal" to have screaming and fighting going on all the time, because of the frenetic energy that we lived through constantly in my young childhood years, walking on eggshells morning, noon and night. When I look back, I'm sure my parents acted out the only way they knew. There was a moment, though, when I realized that I could change my fate and I was determined to do whatever it took to rewire my brain.

When we're conscious of what thoughts we carry, we can change what we bring to ourselves and to the Table of Life. Just because generational patterns are passed down, it doesn't mean that we have to continue carrying these burdens into the future. We can consciously realize that these patterns can be changed for the better.

For me and my family, regardless of the unfortunate situation this presented to us as children, I'm now happy to say that we created pretty wonderful lives in spite of it all. We learned to create our own "Joy Factors" to bring to the Table of our individual lives.

I feel so grateful that I have been able to experience and sustain joy for a long time now and am always thankful that I hover between an 8-10. Sure, childhood cellular memories sometimes get stirred up, and BEing human, I can still go down the rabbit hole. The difference now is that through time I've come to learn, (1) to allow myself to feel the experience without judgment, 2) I am more the "observer" and less the "judge, jury and executioner", and (3) I use certain tools and methods that were taught to me to not stay in that sad pit very long. The goal is always to incrementally shorten up the gap time. I'd much rather hover in the higher part of the Joy Factor Scale, wouldn't you?

At this point and age in my life, I can honestly and joyfully say that the generational chain of abuse stopped with me, which means that the negative ancestral stuff won't be passed on to my grandchildren or their children. This is what success means to me. It's amazing how we can change something in ourselves that outlasts us, like a generational pattern or even a delicious cheesecake recipe handed down from our grandparents. I'll talk more about that in Chapter 11, **in *Living Your Legacy***.

Another way to increase your Joy Factor is to be conscientiously aware of not living your life according to the way you "think others" want you to live your life. Who's doing the cooking?   Who's the chef?   BE aware to not hand anyone the spatula of power over you, thus making someone else responsible for YOUR happiness and Joy Factor. If you do, you may put yourself in a position of constantly seeking approval and validation from others to make sure you are okay.   You may even be living half a life and not even know it. It was once my sour, unsavory recipe! Believe me, that anything I share with you I look inside myself first, then bring my learnings to the Table of Life.

When we are heart-driven and live our lives from the inside out - not based on how "others" want us to live, we live from our own authentic fragrance. Life takes on a whole different flavor, spiced with the seasonings WE want to include. When we are heart-driven, we are in alignment with our heart and mind creating a coherence in our bodies and we get to marinate in that delicious sense of well-being.

When we are heart-driven, we are able to BE more loving, kind, and compassionate, because we are living consciously, rather than BEing ego-driven, wanting, and needing to be right, holding onto and brewing resentment, anger, judgment, impatience, disrespect and other negatively bent ingredients, just because we can, or worse, feel we have to because we're not enough, overcompensating for our feelings of inadequacies. It's akin to over salting food or putting too much spice into something that just overpowers the dish making it inedible.

When we carry thoughts from the past that take us down, we are mixing those thoughts into our now that take us away from being present. When we are consumed with these kinds of thoughts, we're turned backwards walking into our future, thinking our future will be better, but it won't, because we need to turn around and look the other direction, TOWARDS what we want!

When we carry these thoughts into preparing a meal, we're actually not alone in the kitchen because we are carrying whoever else is in those thoughts that are connected with the past, bringing those experiences into our present, and bringing those emotions forward, even souring our experience. It's a no-win situation. Can you see the relation between the thoughts and the patterns that are created from the thoughts?

What good will it do anyone to not live life fully, according to your own soul's journey? Of course, it's your right to blame others for the way in which you live your life, especially if you are miserable and discontent, but that only keeps you hanging out below a 5 on the Joy Factor Scale. Is that where you want to live the majority of your life? It's like living less than half a life, and sorry, but the food you make from this perspective is instilled with all of those limiting sour, icky thoughts, AND you're eating them again and again. Never eat or make food when you are upset. It only can turn to heartburn, just like heartache, when "settling" for less than the quality of life you want and deserve for yourself. We sometimes feel not worthy enough to actually "have" the life we want, so we lower what we want, dim our light for the sake of others, and just "exist". That sounds pretty dim, and not a place where anyone would want to spend any of their precious time, if you ask me.

So, how do you soothe yourself in a way that you can be present and enjoy the process of your life while you are cooking? Yes, you got it, you can pause, stop and do an activity that feeds your inside essence. Here's the next *Happy Mindful Meditation* that will help you soothe your soul and quiet your mind. Two things in one!

Bite Size Re-*Minders* to Living a Yummy Delicious Life

- I remember when I come from love and am heart-driven I am rewiring my brain, creating coherence, and over time, this pattern becomes the norm.
- I remember it takes practice and time to marinate in the right formula.
- I remember to let go of negative thoughts before I cook.
- I remember that I am responsible for my life.
- I remember to live in the moment and be present NOW.

Happy Mindful Meditation #3
Music that Soothes the Soul and Quiets the Mind

In this *Happy Mindful Meditation*, we are going to use sound as a way "in". Sound is another form of energy. Everything everywhere resonates a sound. It is said that OM (AUM) is the original sound of the first echo when the Universe was created, and the light came on and it is present everywhere now. OM (AUM) is the most powerful MANTRA[6] ever. It resonates with the hum of the planet.

Every organ in our body also emits a sound, even though we may not hear it. Sound is a very powerful energy we can use for a multitude of things. We use ultrasound machines to "see" into the body, all through an energetic system that harnesses the energy into a focus. We can also use sound for healing. Have you ever done a "sound bath", where crystal "singing" bowls of various sizes are "played" and you feel the sounds vibrating in your body? It is one of the most sensational experiences I've ever experienced. There is a wonderful place in Joshua Tree, California that I would highly recommend going to enjoy a sound bath experience. It's called the Integratron,[7] and it is a uniquely amazing experience!

In order to receive my yoga teacher's certification when I was in my early twenties, I was required to do a final paper on something I learned. I chose sound vibrations, in which I presented research results of how people healed themselves

---

[6] https://www.google.com/search?q=mantra&oq=mantra&aqs=chrome..69i57j0l7.2469j0j4&sourceid=chrome&ie=UTF-8

[7] https://www.integratron.com/sound-bath/

using sound. Sound vibrations fascinated me and little did I know that I would use it throughout my life to help with my own healing.

I decided to put into practice what I learned about sound vibrations when I gave birth to my daughter in 1979. The nurses were quite astounded by what they were witnessing and what I was demonstrating. Every contraction I had, I made an "ooooooh" sound that resonated with the first energy center (chakra)[8] in my body, and the birthing experience was intentional and simply amazing! My eyes were closed, and I felt at one with my breath, my sound, my baby, my body, and my mind, not to mention how open my heart was, giving birth and life to a baby human!

The type of music you listen to also affects your energy and has an impact on how you feel. I know for me, when I listen to a piece of soothing, meditative music, it allows me to take a deep breath and flow with the music, feeling relaxed and in alignment with myself and the Universe. I hope you enjoy your *Happy Mindful Meditation.*

- Find a quiet comfortable place, ensuring yourself that your time and space are regarded without interruption.
- Sit comfortably and begin BEing conscious of your breathing. Just focus on your breath, inhaling and exhaling, noticing how you take in air and how you release air.
- Listen to one of your favorite pieces of instrumental music: classical symphony, smooth jazz, meditation music, etc. whatever is soothing to you.
- Focus on the flow of the music and how it takes you up, around, down, higher and deeper.

---

[8] https://en.wikipedia.org/wiki/Chakra

- Take note of what essence the musical flow awakens in you.

- Sit with the music for just a moment or two, and even take 5 minutes if you want. Go ahead and indulge. It's your time. You're worth it.

Going Inward Before the Meal

How did the music make you feel? Where did it take you? Identify one essence that came to the surface. Keep alive in your mind what essence came up for you. You are now ready to bring the energy of that essence to your cooking and to the Table of Life.

_____

_____

_____

_____

Shelley's Famous BBQ Glazed Salmon

Making salmon is probably one of my all-time favorites. I usually make more than I will eat in one sitting, because I love leftovers that I can use either in tossed salads or making my own salmon salad mixture with mayo and chopped celery and can eat it cold the next day straight from the container while I'm writing. I love salmon slightly undercooked. Every time I make it for my guests, they love it too, so, any way you want to eat it, enjoy the taste!

Serves 4
Prep time: 10 minutes
Cook time: 12 minutes
Total time: 22 minutes

Ingredients

2 pounds boneless salmon fillets
½ cup TJ's Brown Sugar BBQ Sauce
1 Tbs honey
2 Tbs Worchester Sauce
2 Tbs balsamic glaze
1 Tbs Gourmet Garden Ginger Paste
1 Tbs Gourmet Garden Lemon Grass Paste
1 tsp minced garlic
1 tsp grated ginger
3 Tbs extra virgin olive oil
1 tsp Everything but the Bagel Seasoning
Pinch of salt
Pinch of pepper

Method

Cut up into portions and take out of the refrigerator for at least 15 minutes prior to cooking

In a small shallow bowl, mix the BBQ Sauce, honey, minced garlic, olive oil, ginger paste, lemon grass paste, and grated ginger. Stir to get mixture smooth

Add salmon and turn on both sides, letting the salmon marinate, while preparing the rest of the meal

Heat a nonstick skillet/pan over medium heat with 2 Tbs olive oil

Cook salmon 5 to 6 minutes on each side, until fish begins to flake with a fork, and remove it from the pan

We serve it with my grandchildren's favorite Crispy Broccoli recipe

Jake, Jordyn & Zoe's Favorite Crispy Broccoli

All my grandchildren love broccoli, zucchini and Brussel sprouts, and to crisp it up, it adds a fun factor. Here is a very simple recipe for Crispy Broccoli.

Serves 4
Prep time: 10 minutes
Cook time: 15-20 minutes
Total time: 25-30 minutes

Ingredients

2 lbs. broccoli tops
3 tbs extra virgin olive oil
Pinch of salt
Pinch of garlic powder
Everything But the Bagel Seasoning

Method

Preheat oven to 400

Put the broccoli tops in a gallon size baggy

Pour extra virgin olive oil into the baggy

Close the baggy really well with the air out and smoosh the olive oil around the broccoli until coated evenly

Pour out the broccoli onto a cookie sheet covered with tinfoil

Season with salt, garlic powder, and Everything But the Bagel Seasoning

Bake for about 10 minutes, turning the broccoli over half-way, then bake for another 10 minutes

Hit the broiler at the end for extra crispness. It's really yum!

Going Inward After the Meal

Music always has a way of soothing the soul and calming the mind, as we've talked about. Write down how this Happy Mindful Meditation of listening to your favorite music impacted the way you cooked. Did you notice anything different? Did the essence permeate your experience? Did you enjoy the process? What was the result? Your takeaway? Any reactions from family and friends?

Self-Reflections/Notes

Chapter 4
Family & Friends: Relationships

"Dining with one's friends and beloved family is certainly one of life's primal and most innocent delights, one that is both soul-satisfying and eternal".

-Julia Child

There is nothing better than having a trusted friend, family member, or anyone else you know, give you love and receive your love unconditionally. It's like relying on one of your favorite foods from your refrigerator or pantry that you know without a doubt, tastes delicious and just hits the spot time and time again. I freeze bananas when they are "almost" ripe. If I'm in the mood, I'll just go to the freezer, take out one of those Saran-wrapped bananas and eat it like ice cream. It always hits the spot!

It's a blessing to have an authentic and true relationship with family and friends, and that special bond of love is one of the greatest formulas we can consume together at the community/collective table. However, the most important relationship is the one that starts with yourself, the hearty connection between your human and your soul. When you have a healthy relationship within, feeling a sense of connection, harmony and coherence between your heart, your mind, your body and your soul, you are full of nourishing essences to share with others that are genuine. You are then able to give genuinely to someone else's life with sincere intention.

Sometimes, as we learn about having healthy relationships, we experience some lumps in the mixture and it's not always a creamy, smooth consistency. Have you ever been in a relationship where your appetite to express your feelings was not equal, and you wanted to "change" that person, but they were not open to change? Did you ever think that your love was the secret ingredient that could melt their heart and they would open and "be" the way you want them to be? Well, I learned an extremely valuable lesson and the symbol for this life healing is a **can opener**. Why a can opener you might ask? Because I swore that I would never pry someone's heart open again if they didn't want it opened. Whenever I look at that can opener, I am always Re-*Minded* that I need to focus on what energy I bring to the Table and not get someone else to change or open up if they don't want to nor choose to do so.

Yes, I know, we hurt each other at times with our words and our actions, but remember, we are human. When we are able to accept and admit OUR part in the situation, we are able to heal whatever is going on, or at least we can heal within ourselves. We don't have control over anybody else.

There are three "F" words that I want to address here, (no, not *those* "F" words. LOL), and they are: *Forgiveness, Fingerpointyitus*, and *Friends for Life*.

Forgiveness: When you *forgive* someone (or yourself) for "hurting you", you are healing something inside of YOU and you are changing the chemical cocktail to a love frequency. You are releasing resentment and harsh feelings of judgment. When you don't forgive, you are the one who suffers, because all of that judgment stays INSIDE of you, like foods that go sour and ferment in your gut. Your body remembers the negative emotion by the chemicals it produces and eventually your body becomes addicted to the feelings/sensations of the chemicals that are running throughout your body. Be careful what you allow to run rampant in your body.

Have you ever taken something out of the refrigerator that you forgot was in there and it smelled up your whole kitchen from being putrid? That's what is happening emotionally, physically and mentally inside of you when you don't clean out your own "refrigerator or pantry" that is holding your information. Maybe the feelings have been frozen inside of you and you were so numb to them, you didn't even notice how they have been affecting you since childhood! Maybe those feelings had an expiration date that you didn't pay attention to and they run your life unknowingly.

Chemically speaking, when you have thoughts that emit negative emotions, your brain emits the appropriate chemicals and it becomes a self-fulfilling prophecy that just keeps going around and around. The neural pathways form a loop in the brain that keep emitting the chemicals that keep us feeling negative. We continually look for any evidence that supports that negativity and the cycle and pattern continues. The body becomes "addicted" to its own chemicals,[9] and until we find a way to STOP the pattern, we will just continue to go down the rabbit hole. It's like being addicted to and craving greasy fried foods.

The second "F" word is *"Fingerpointyitus"*. I made this word up, based on a disease that I've observed that seems to afflict most people. It's pointing the finger out and blaming others for how you feel. It's the good old, "If you would only change, I would feel better," syndrome. It's taking that spatula or baton of power I spoke of earlier, giving it to someone else, and making them responsible for how you feel, for your emotional, mental and spiritual well-being. That's not only not fair (another "f" word), but it takes away the responsibility for your own self. It's silly, because then you never take responsibility for your life, and you've stopped being the

---

[9] https://blog.drjoedispenza.com/evolve-your-brain

CEO (remember, Chief Energy Officer) of your own circumstances and state of well-being.

The third "F" word is what I call, "*Friends for Life*". This is a special way that we approach relationships. It comes with a set of agreements on how to "BE" with each other: 1) Each person takes responsibility for his/her own experience, from one human being to another and has the courage to express what is really going on inside, from one human being to another, feeling safe in revealing and sharing what's going on inside. 2) The traditional roles we play are set aside: (partners/boyfriend/girlfriend, husband/wife/partners, parent/child, friends, etc.). 3) Each person holds the space for each other to have their human experience without judgment. 4) Each person brings honor, dignity and regard to the Table of Life. 5) Each person is supportive of each other and makes it a point to uplift, rather than criticize or tear down. 6) Because every relationship has a form that can change, each person accepts that even if the form (another "f" word) of the relationship can change, the friendship will remain, regardless of the form. Does this make sense?

It is so satisfying and satiating to have a healthy relationship. Who wants to walk on eggshells with anyone at any time? I grew up in a house where everyone walked on eggshells, and take it from me, it is no fun at all. It breeds stress and bitter feelings where nothing anyone does is ever enough, knowing that someone is doing something wrong for something. "I'm going to get in trouble," used to be my daily mantra as a child and even spilled into adulthood many times. Changing it to, "I feel full of possibility," is so much better, wouldn't you say?

Bite Size Re-*Minders* to Living a Yummy Delicious Life

- I remember to nourish my relationships, starting with the one I have with myself.

- I remember never to pry someone's heart open if they don't want it opened.

- I remember to accept other people's perspective and hold the space for them to have their human experience without judgment.

- I remember to forgive others and myself for being human and making mistakes.

- I remember to not point the finger out and blame others for how I feel and to take full responsibility for how I show up and what I am experiencing.

Happy Mindful Meditation #4
Choosing one of your favorite photos inspiring wonderful memories

Wonderful memories with family and friends stimulate our senses and fill our hearts with an immeasurable amount of love. Photos capture the moments you experienced, whether at a holiday party, on one of your favorite vacations or just posing at home.

The photo is a snapshot of ONE moment in time in your life with someone you love, and if they are no longer in the physical realm, maybe the photo gives you a sense of strength, knowing that person loved and believed in you, and you loved and believed in them. It takes a split second to bring those memories back, just by using your eyes and your mind.

I did this exercise looking at a photo of two of my best friends of 35 years, Toni and Gene Bua, who passed away 4 years apart. They were married for 44 years. They lived a fairy tale life, being soap opera stars together and one of the most talented writing/composing teams ever. They were truly each other's muse. In the last 6 years of Toni's life, I was privileged to be her and her husband, Gene's guardian and life coach.

Whenever I made Toni food, she would always say, "Shelley, this is the BEST food ever." She always loved the food I made her. When food is made with love, it almost doesn't matter what you make.

Let yourself have those precious moments to reset your heart dial into a place of love, letting yourself be in the moment, which is cooking with excited intention in the kitchen. I hope you enjoy your *Happy Mindful Meditation.*

- Find a quiet comfortable place, ensuring yourself that your time and space are regarded without interruption.

- Sit comfortably and begin being conscious of your breathing. Just focus on your breath, inhaling and exhaling, noticing how you take in air and how you release air.

- As you take a deep breath, gaze upon one of your favorite photos that brings you a sense of joy.

- Let yourself remember the wonderful memories that come up.

- Picture yourself wherever the photo was taken with the person who you were with and bask in those memories and fill yourself up with the love you feel for that person.

- Let the experience come alive within you.

- Say a note of gratitude for the experience.

Going Inward Before the Meal

Remembering something wonderful, bring that feeling into the kitchen and into the meal you are about to make. What essences have come to the surface from gazing at one of your favorite photos? You are now ready to bring the energy of that essence to your cooking and to the Table of Life.

_____

_____

_____

_____

Shelley's Savory & Sweet Turkey Meatloaf

If you like meatloaf, this turkey meatloaf recipe is fantastic! It's sweet and sour and savory delicious! It's really one of my favorite turkey meatloaves on the planet. Don't overcook it, because it will be dry. I've added some nice creamy mashed potatoes as a side dish. Feel free to pour the sauce into the mashed potatoes like gravy. I'm telling you, it's really tasty!

Serves 6-8
Prep time: 30 minutes
Cook time: 35 minutes
Total time: 65 minutes

Ingredients

Sauce:
2 16 oz cans tomato sauce
3 14.5 oz cans diced tomatoes
1 6 oz can of tomato paste
1/3 cup packed brown sugar
¼ cup golden raisins
3 Tbs olive oil
3 Tbs lemon juice
2 bay leaves and remove before eating

Meatloaf mix:
2 lbs. ground turkey
2 pkgs onion soup mix
3 eggs
1 11.5-oz. can V-8 juice
½ cup breadcrumbs/panko

Method

For Sauce:
Put all ingredients in a 5-quart pot Cook over low heat until sauce is simmering nicely together. Taste to see if you want to add more lemon juice or brown sugar. I like to put in at least 2 bay leaves, but again, this is your preference.

For Meatloaf:
Preheat oven to 350F.
Put all ingredients in a big bowl.
Wearing food prep gloves, mix together with hands, so all ingredients are mixed in well.
Keep turkey meatloaf mixture in the refrigerator, while you are making the sauce.
When sauce is ready, take out the meatloaf mixture and set on the counter.
In a 9x11 lasagna pan, pour some of the sauce in the bottom of the pan.
Shape the turkey meat mixture into a meatloaf form.
Pour remaining sauce on top.
Put in oven.

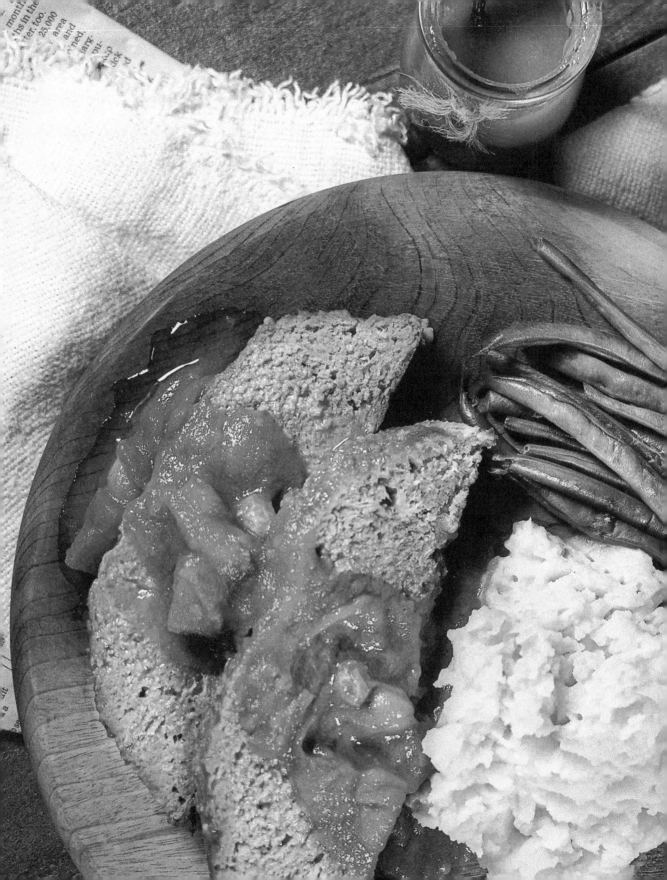

Creamy Dreamy Mashed Potatoes

I don't know anyone who doesn't like creamy dreamy mashed potatoes and so simple to make. This is one of my family's favorite mashed potato recipes, so make it with love and go ahead and splurge on the butter, just this one time.

Serves 6-8
Total Prep time: 20 minutes
Cook time: 15-20 minutes
Total time: 40 minutes

Ingredients

12 medium russet potatoes, washed, peeled & chopped
1 cup of warm whole milk
6-12 Tbs melted temperature butter
1 tsp salt or to taste
Pinch of pepper
1 Tbs finely chopped fresh parsley or chives

Method

Place washed, peeled & chopped potatoes in a large pot (5Qt+) and cover with cold water at least an inch covering the potatoes. Add salt.

Bring to a boil. Reduce heat to low/simmer and cook partially covered for 15-20 minutes until easily pierced with a fork.

While potatoes are cooking, melt butter and milk together.

Drain cooked potatoes. Mash the potatoes with a potato masher or electric hand mixer, pour in the warm milk/butter mixture slowly and keep mixing, stirring, mashing (Don't overmix, otherwise potatoes get gummy).

Add any salt and pepper to taste.

Going Inward After the Meal

Looking at photos can conjure up wonderful memories. Take a moment to write down what essence you brought into your experience of cooking after you allowed yourself those few moments of remembering someone you loved. Did you bring them with you into the kitchen while you were cooking? Did you have a smile on your face and in your heart while thinking about them? How did the Deep-Dive into the discovery of your essence affect your cooking? Was it enjoyable? Any comments from family and friends?

Self-Reflections/Notes

_____

_____

_____

_____

_____

_____

_____

_____

_____

_____

_____

_____

Chapter 5
Love, Love, Love

"Love is the greatest power, it is, if natural,
the highest invisible food from the infinite for soul and body."
-Arnold Ehret

What is it about Love that makes everything feel better, and even taste better? Love in itself is pure in its essence, I believe, and unconditional love is love in its highest essence. To love and to feel loved are two of the greatest and most satisfying/ gratifying experiences one can have. To give love without judgment, cause, or expectation, is one of the most exquisite essences you can bring to the Table of Life.

Lovers celebrate over dinner, lovers cook together and no matter how it turns out, they deem it delicious. Love is the glue of humanity. Everything is born of love. Love is powerful, courageous, brave, strong, beautiful and healthy for the soul. Love has the power to heal and forgive too, allowing the pain to subside as we forgive for each other.

When I say, "Remember to bring love into everything you do," I mean everything. Cooking without love and desire will never taste as yummy delicious as when you put love, heart and desire into it, as with everything you do in life. The energy and the spirit of love you put in your dish nurtures your body and your soul. Without the ingredient of love, it barely feeds your body.

I heard a statement years ago in one of the courses I took that rang true to my soul, "How you do anything is how you do everything." Boy, now that's a powerful statement that stops you in your tracks, and makes you think about what you are bringing to your experience!

One time I was walking from my bedroom to my living room and I saw a small piece of paper on the floor. I walked right by it. Then, I turned on my heels and picked up that piece of paper. Sometimes, we walk right by something so unconsciously, we don't even "see" what we're bypassing. I love my home/ sanctuary that I created, so leaving that piece of paper on the floor was not a loving thing to do. I've got a whole lot to say about creating a loving space that supports you, and I'll talk about that in Chapter 6, **Creating Your Sanctuary**. When we bring love to the table, we bring our consciousness of the boundless spirit that emanates from the Universe of which we are part. I cannot imagine life without love. They just go together like peanut butter and jelly. "Life and Love!" Hmmm, has a nice ring to it, right?

Love also inspires, ignites, and is a catalyst for more love. Love is the gift that keeps on giving and grows with more love. Love spreads kindness, respect, and regard. Love appreciates. Love cares and shows compassion for humanity. Love is just. Love transcends boundaries of time and space and outlives any human. Love transforms, uplifts, and brings joy, happiness and, remember, more love. Love can be seen and tasted in the food we make for those we love. Have you ever felt a small "ping" when someone doesn't like what you made? It feels as though they don't love you. I know for me, I have to constantly let go of my "expectation" that someone will just love what I make for them, because I made it with love.

As much as we are wired for impending danger, we are also wired for love, to assure the continuation of our species. We are created in love to assure procreation so that we can survive and grow. Love shows its innocence through the miracle of being able to create a whole new life, a brand-new baby human. Love is Love and is said to be the impetus of all creation. How else would we be able to make it through the first year that a baby is born? No one gets any sleep and sleep deprivation can run havoc on one's system, but it's LOVE that gets us through.

Thousands of books have been written about love. Poets, writers, philosophers and lovers all write about love. Marianne Williamson wrote a wonderful book, called, "Return to Love", a superb expose about love being your home to return to as a safe haven.

Love is an energy field that draws us to it. Love can be diminished, however and sometimes we fall "out" of love, but a deeper "unconditional" love can still exist, even though we may not be "in love" with the same person anymore. Just as energy, love itself cannot be destroyed, it can only change form. Some people may use "God" as another word/concept for Love. Love is spirit. Love IS (like energy IS). So, I've added another word to my delicious recipe for life, Energy = Spirit = Love. When we feel connected to that magical "something" that is so much bigger than ourselves, we FEEL LOVE in every pore of our being.

I believe we all have the potential to be generators of love/energy/spirit when we feel connected to that higher, more universal energy of "All That Is". When we let ourselves remember that we are part of this grander picture, we feel part of this loving nature. It's acknowledging to ourselves that when we surrender to that infinite light that is eternal and loving, we reach the realization that we too are made of this "divine" substance that's made up of light that works through, for and as "us". The light can bring forth healing, wellness and truth in our own energy fields, into every cell of our being, and with every breath we take. When we allow ourselves to be a channel of this grander love, we are ever present with this love.

The key word here is "allow". When we allow ourselves to be a channel of love, we tap into this unlimited supply of energy, much like a well that is always full of fresh water. When we feel a sense of well-being, we can feel love. Well-being and love can heal every part of our existence as they also radiate onto others.

When you bring this kind of unconditional love essence to the Table of Life and into your kitchen when you are cooking, the love ingredients seep into the food and you can feel it when you eat. Love is palpable. Sprinkle it, dash it, or use gobs of it in everything you cook.

Bite Size Re-*Minders* to Living a Yummy Delicious Life

- I remember that love is the magic healing elixir, standing the test of time.

- I remember to bring love into everything I do.

- I remember to allow myself to be loving, loveable and loved.

- I remember that love IS the energy that grows all things, beats our hearts and breathes our bodies.

- I remember that love is the gift that keeps on giving.

Happy Mindful Meditation #5
Relaxing on an Exotic Beach or Peaceful Island

Love is the magic healing elixir of all time and imagining is one of the greatest gifts given to human beings. As humans, we have the ability to go into the past and into the future, just using our imagination, which is the co-creative center with *All That Is (the universal, quantum field of possibilities)*. Using your imagination for something wonderful is a constructive and delightful way of taking advantage of this gift you were given. No other animal in the world is able to imagine the past or the future. Humans are unique in that way.

Traveling to exotic places in the world is one of the advantages we have without ever having to buy a ticket. We can imagine and travel to our favorite places all in the comfort of our own homes using our minds. Take advantage of this *Happy Mindful Meditation* and let yourself BE wherever your mind takes you. I hope you enjoy your mindful moment.

- Find a quiet comfortable place, ensuring yourself that your time and space are regarded without interruption.
- Sit comfortably and begin being conscious of your breathing. Just focus on your breath, inhaling and exhaling, noticing how you take in air and how you release air.

- Take a nice deep breath, filling your belly with your life force, inhaling and exhaling. Keep the breath flowing.
- Gently allow yourself to close your eyes.
- Envision yourself relaxing on a beach or exotic island somewhere you have been or have always wanted to go.
- Let yourself smell the ocean air.
- Let yourself hear the sounds of the waves gently washing ashore.
- Feel the gentle breeze on your skin.
- Feel the sun warming your body. It's the perfect temperature, not too hot and not too cold.
- Look up at the beautiful blue sky with a few puffy clouds floating by.
- Feel yourself totally relaxed in this place.
- Feel a sense of gratitude enter your heart and let it expand.
- Now gently bring yourself back into the room you are in and take another nice deep breath, feeling refreshed and rejuvenated.

Going Inward Before the Meal

How did that make you feel? What was it like to be transported to a beautiful place? Identify one essence that came to the surface. Keep alive in your mind what essence came up for you. You are now ready to bring the energy of that essence to your cooking and the Table of Life.

_____

_____

_____

_____

The Shirley Whizin Killer Hershey Chocolate Cake

Who doesn't love chocolate? Chocolate has been lovers' delight for centuries. This is a fool proof recipe and was passed down from the Whizin side of the family. I'm telling you, no matter what I have done to this recipe, it always comes out DELICIOUS! You'll see! You just can't kill it!

Serves 8
Prep time: 20 minutes
Bake time: 35 minutes
Total time: 55 minutes

Ingredients

¼ lb. salted butter (room temperature)
¾ cup of sugar
4 eggs (room temperature)
1 cup sifted flour
1 tsp baking powder
Dash of salt
1 lg can of Hershey chocolate syrup
1 tsp vanilla

Method

Preheat oven to 350 degrees

Cream butter and sugar

Add the eggs

Sift flour, baking powder and salt together, set aside.

Add the sifted dry ingredients (on slow speed if using an electric mixer) to wet ingredients with can of Hershey chocolate syrup, vanilla, and mix until creamy.

Pour into a 9" greased floured Pyrex dish or Bundt pan.

Bake at 350 for 35 minutes.

When cool, frost with favorite icing or just sprinkle some powdered sugar on top or drip the Hershey syrup all over it. This will keep moist if refrigerated (Reminder: you cannot kill this cake, even if you burn it. I'm telling you it will taste delicious no matter what).

Going Inward After the Meal

Now that you brought the experience of being on an exotic island, or wherever your favorite place took you, into the flavor of your cooking, take a moment to write down how this impacted your cooking experience. Were you more relaxed? Did you have more fun while cooking? Was the process enjoyable? How was the Deep-Dive into the discovery of your essence? Was it satisfying? Was it enjoyable? Any comments from family and friends?

Self-Reflections/Notes

_____

_____

_____

_____

_____

_____

_____

_____

_____

_____

_____

_____

_____

Chapter 6
Creating your Sanctuary

"Food feeds our souls. It is the single great unifier across all cultures.
The table offers a sanctuary and a place to come together for unity and
understanding."
-Lidia Bastianich

Our place of dwelling is more important to our sense of spiritual well-being than we often recognize. How we live reflects our inner heart and home is our place of solace, comfort, refuge, and support. It's our precious abode, and when we walk through that door, we want to feel a warm "welcome" and loved up just to be there. We can change the energy from "happenstance" to "intentional living" when we bring things that we love into our home.

A few years ago, I brought furniture into my new place that reflected the twenty years of marriage after I divorced, because I just wanted to "keep" everything the way it was. I also was attached to the customized desk and cabinet that I had personally designed and had made whilst married. The furniture I brought from my previous married life home to my new single one "fit" less and less with me as time went on. I wasn't even in touch with what my "style" was now that I was in my new single identity.

By the time I decided to move to another apartment, I realized that I didn't have to live according to someone else's style, so I decided to let go and change everything. I started with taking a good "heart" look, going inside and examining myself and was then able let go of any objects that held a negative energy or memory, regardless of how beautiful the object was.   Holding on to old life stuff made me question what was I bringing to the table of my own life through that style?   In going down deep into myself, I became empowered to create a true reflection of my heart and identity in my new home making it a sanctuary!

Every single thing in my home now, has a loving energy, and every single time I open my door, I immediately feel comforted, soothed and loved up. I love coming home, and now, as I write this book in quarantine, due to the pandemic of Covid-19, I'm so grateful I have this beautiful home to be cocooning in.

It's not about how big the space is, it's what we bring into that space that matters, and the first ingredient is LOVE (and joy right along with love). Furthermore, just from the nature of the work of being a life coach, teacher, hospice trainer and end of life doula/guide, I knew I needed a place where I could completely unwind, feel supported and be "held". As I designed and decorated my home, I made sure that love was the main ingredient in all that I did through the colors, shapes, and decor that resonated with my heart, creating a sense of harmony and easy fluidity. I love my bedroom furniture, and my king-sized bed with its velvet tufted headboard, and aqua blue wall behind my bed - the sanctuary feel of my bedroom makes me feel like a queen!

Changing things in your space helps to heal experiences you may not even have known needed healing. Sometimes bad experiences from childhood or a soured relationship involving arguments, pose a challenge to turn it around and make it your sanctuary. After my friend, Toni's husband died, she wanted to redo her kitchen. Her kitchen was extremely disorganized as nothing had a consistent designated place. Although she wanted to change it, she had great resistance in changing it. I later found out why.

When she was a child, her parents used to fight in the kitchen and throw dishes at each other in their fights. Therefore, the kitchen brought up such terrible memories for Toni. I helped her reframe those old memories and brought her to create it as the heart of the home, instead of a room that reflected frighteningly horrible childhood memories. Toni's whole perspective changed, and she looked forward to going into her kitchen. She was able to enjoy her kitchen for another 3 years before she died. I'm so happy that she healed her childhood experiences, and we got to love her up and her home in that way.

Creating a sanctuary is important to your spirit. It reflects your heart, and your home needs to be your place where you get to take charge of what charges you. Surround yourself with pieces that you love, so you fill your place with a sense of peace.

Also, a gentle reminder to choose how your home is lit. Is your house dimly lit, or do you have bright lights? Dimmers are a great way to allow choices according to your mood. You want to make sure that you're not living with dim lighting to reflect any dimness in your life's light.

Have fun designing/creating your home sanctuary. Fill it gently with things that speak to your heart. Plants are a great and inexpensive way to give life and color to your home. You deserve love. You deserve to make your place your very own sanctuary that loves you back. When you walk in the door of your home, you will feel that you're walking into an energy that is comforting, loving and supportive to your sense of peace.

Remember that your home needs to be your very own sanctuary. The moment you walk in the door, you take a deep breath, feel loved up, and supported by its beauty. It's a reflection of your heart.

Bite Size Re-*Minders* to Living a Yummy Delicious Life

- I remember that my home is a reflection of my heart. I will only bring in objects that I love.
- I remember my home is my sanctuary, a place of comfort, solace and support.
- I remember to let go of any object that carries negative energy.
- I remember that I deserve to live in a loving environment.
- I remember to have fun in my own home, that it is a place of joy.

Happy Mindful Meditation #6
Gratitude and Appreciation

Now that you know why it is so important to create a safe, beautiful sanctuary, it is time to look around, scan and appreciate everything that you have. Everything tells a story.

Your environment reflects a sense of beauty that you hold in your heart. Appreciate yourself through the stories that exist in every object you scan. Feel a sense of gratitude for having the opportunity of bringing yourself on the journey of your life.

I hope you enjoy your *Happy Mindful Meditation.*

- Find a quiet comfortable place, ensuring yourself that your time and space are regarded without interruption.
- Sit comfortably and begin being conscious of your breathing. Just focus on your breath, inhaling and exhaling, noticing how you take in air and how you release air.
- Gaze around the room and just look at all of the beautiful things you have.
- Send everything you have a sense of appreciation.
- Focus on one object that brings you particular joy in this moment.
- Let yourself remember the story behind the object. Feel the joy of the experience and send it appreciation.
- Thank all of your things in your home for bringing you a sense of joy.

Going Inward Before the Meal

How did you feel going around the room looking at the beauty of your environment? Focus only on the items that gave you strong positive vibes. Identify one essence that came to you as you gazed on one of your precious items. Keep alive in your mind and note the essence came up for you. You are now ready to bring the energy of that essence to your cooking and the Table of Life.

_____

_____

_____

_____

Jordyn's Jiving Avocado Toast Tapenade

My granddaughter, Jordyn, loves avocados, especially avocado toast. Here's one of her favorite recipes. She's a budding cook herself, as she, Jake, Zoe and I all like to watch Chopped on TV together and create our own recipes. When they were younger, they would be the judges, put foods in a brown paper bag for me to create something, and as they got older, I did the same for them. We've had such a fun time creating food together in the kitchen. Try it on for an experience with your children and family. It's really fun! ENJOY!

Serves 4
Prep time: 20 minutes

Ingredients

3 ripe avocados, pitted & scooped

24 small pitted black olives, drained

2 tsp finely chopped fresh cilantro

3 tsp lemon juice

4 Persian cucumbers, peeled & finely chopped

10 cherry tomatoes, chopped into small pieces

Pinch of Everything but the Bagel Seasoning

Handful of greens, finely chopped

4 pieces of sourdough bread toasted

Method

In a food processor, combine the olives, avocado, cilantro and lemon, and pulse until smooth. Spread the tapenade on the sourdough toast, top with the cucumber, chopped tomatoes, chopped greens, and serve.

Going Inward After the Meal

Gratitude and appreciation are such beautiful sensations/essences for human beings to experience. How did this particular Deep-Dive in going around the room and appreciating what you have tap into the essence you brought into the kitchen? Take a moment to write what you discovered in the process. Was it helpful? Enjoyable? Did it spark memories you hadn't thought of in a long time, and what was the result? Did the essence change as you were cooking? How was it for you?

Self-Reflections/Notes

Chapter 7
Change Your Thoughts, Change Your Life

"All you need is love. But a little chocolate now and then doesn't hurt."

-Charles M. Schulz

I love a good sense of humor, and I think it's great not to take ourselves so seriously that we strip the very joy out of life, or a meal. When we appreciate good humor, we can grow to sometimes let go. This chapter will give you a taste of the human/ spiritual dynamic that has gone on almost since the beginning of time, and how we have evolved.

Changing a thought seems like such an easy thing to do, like changing an ingredient in a recipe, and yet changing a thought is known to be one of the most challenging things to do. However, because of several factors I'll expose, it is possible.

We humans are creatures of habit, and the negative or un-serving thoughts we think over and over again form a pattern, which become part of our neural pathway system, and the body eventually "becomes the mind",[10] losing control of our conscious thoughts. Imagine a body snatcher swooping in and taking over. The body acts like a robot and we just go on automatic, not even aware of what we are thinking

---

[10] Breaking the Habit of Being Yourself by Dr. Joe Dispenza, page 2

half the time. We wake up and we get out of the bed from the same side. We check our phones, and everything is pretty much the same as it was yesterday.

If we are engaged in a consistent thought loop where we feel "bad" about things in our life, then chances are that this consistency of negative mind talk/thinking becomes a thought pattern. Our mind thus becomes badly "trained" and goes into that negative thought pattern without even thinking, as if it's our "normal". These are also tied into our childhood memories of what we thought "normal" was.

Until we make a conscious decision and effort to break away from our old thought patterns as well as some beliefs that continue to limit us in our sense of well-being, we will stay "stuck" in these patterns. This state can block out that sense of daily joy in living and well-being even though everything may not be perfect. Why do you suppose these thought patterns get turned around? You may have heard that "Energy flows where attention goes", or, any similar adaptation. Therefore, the negative mind talk pattern signals the brain to then have the body secrete particular hormones that result in "feeling" a certain way from those types of habitual thoughts. Then, whatever we think becomes a reality and the loop just keeps going around and around. This puts the onus on the physical and you end up being a victim of circumstance (living from the outside in, victim mentality).

When you take a sincere Deep-Dive into yourself and see the beliefs and paradigms that don't seem to be working for you, most likely these need to be faced, and once you're aware of them, you can take your second step. This is what it means to take charge of what's inside of you. The brain responds by secreting certain hormones, like cortisol and adrenaline, and other stress hormones that make the body run on automatic in those mind frames. I call these "body snatchers", because your body has been trained and accustomed to run as if on automatic.

Feel your body when you're stressed. Do you feel "sick" in your stomach? Is your asthma exacerbated? Are the people around you reacting to your "energy" in a negative way? When you're aware of even one thing, you can then make the decision to not bring it in the food you're making. You can now change what you're bringing into your food, and to your table when you eat it.

These are not really "new" concepts. Albert Einstein proclaimed that energy and matter are fundamentally related, as one and the same, completely interchangeable.[11] This thinking shifted the belief that thoughts not only matter, they definitely change the way in which our bodies respond to our thoughts, thus changing our lives. When you practice staying aware of your thoughts often enough, you are now bringing this shift to the table of life too. Doing this sets you up to live from the inside out, no longer a victim, once the cause of reality.

Now that you've become consciously aware of your old beliefs and paradigms the work continues to replace those with ones that serve, uplift, are more philosophically positive, and inspire you to take the actions required to give you the compelling awareness. The challenge is to have that realization that the new beliefs may not fit into your old perceptions of what you had originally been believing as "reality". It's about being open with yourself about what you believe, because it may be based on a faulty belief system. Full conscious awareness leads to fundamental shifts in your understanding in order to change your life. It's like rubbing your eyes and then little by little seeing clearly and discerning your belief systems and faulty based "thinking". Examples are plenty. One poignant example is echoing the same things your parents may have said long ago that came from their story, their experiences, their time in life, and even thought patterns they themselves inherited

---

[11] https://en.wikipedia.org/wiki/Mass%E2%80%93energy_equivalence

from their own parents. Some are good, strong values, and others could be negatively geared, and some are just faulty.

We have all read about the time, we believed the earth was flat. The belief held by our historical ancestors was that if they ventured out too far, they would fall off the edge of the earth into an endless abyss. This is an example of faulty thinking stemming from lack of experience and knowledge. To grapple with notions unseen, the physical/material realm was perceived as being more "real" than the un-perceived invisible/spiritual realm. The point is that changing your perspective about your experience will help you to shift thought patterns that are based on faulty paradigms. In a way it's normal to resist change, because beliefs can be so deeply engrained in our psyche, that it's sometimes hard to see the truth beneath ideas, thoughts and paradigms. We suppressed citizens because of their race, gender and religion. The truth is that we are all human beings with the right to thrive in society.

Changing a recipe is a piece of cake. You can add this ingredient and eliminate that ingredient, creating something that tastes different than any one recipe you used as your basic frame of reference. When it comes to changing your recipe for living a happy, joyful and meaningful life, it can be a little more involved because you've got to Deep-Dive within yourself and see yourself truthfully – which parts are you, and which parts are from authority figures and environments of the past.

Therefore, energy is the very fabric of all things material and is responsive to the mind, as we talked about in Chapter 2, **Energy: The Boundless Spirit.**

Keep in mind that, as humans, we have the ability to think thoughts that can literally freak us right out, pounding our hearts out of whack, raising our blood pressure, heartbeat and constricting blood vessels affecting the sympathetic and parasympathetic nervous systems, which are great in the face of danger, but run havoc on a daily basis. Think of the sympathetic nervous system as the gas pedal in a car. It just goes. Think of the parasympathetic nervous system as the brakes. It wants to stop and rest. If we go too long having our foot on the pedal, we not only get more stressed out, we get exhausted because the adrenaline is rushing into our bodies to save us from danger. Many times, there is no "real" danger, but danger we have made up from a place of fear. The body then responds, and to boot becomes addicted to its own chemicals. Go figure!

Needless to say, this causes tremendous distress on the body physically, psychologically and emotionally, by creating a chain reaction of stress chemicals of cortisol, adrenaline, epinephrine, that run throughout the body, igniting our fight or flight reptilian brain, and compromise the immune system.[12] Then we can equally think thoughts that heal us and make us well, emitting the "feel good" chemicals like endorphins, serotonin, oxytocin and dopamine. Equal rights to energy expended.

When you change your thoughts consciously, your mind stays in control. When you let your body run the kitchen, so to speak, your body just simply responds like a robot, reacting to the chemicals that are running rampant throughout your system. If you are hosting feelings of anger, frustration, anxiety, fear or any survival emotions, your body, becomes familiar with its addiction to your own chemicals and you continue to find outside evidence to keep yourself in the reality you have created. That is exhausting!

As I mentioned above, it takes a conscious awareness of your thoughts and an understanding that with practice, you can change the way in which you operate. You can look at what you want, instead of looking at what you have experienced over and over and focus on elevating your emotions based on experiences you desire and not

---

[12] https://www.health.harvard.edu/staying-healthy/understanding-the-stress-response

focusing on experiences from the past that make you feel bad over and over again. That's another reason I offer the *Happy Mindful Meditations*, just to practice what it feels like to change your mindset from being stressed out to a sense of well-being. I sincerely hope you enjoy this next exercise.

Bite Size Re-*Minders* to Living a Yummy Delicious Life

- I remember that it is within my power to change any faulty beliefs/paradigms.
- I remember that my energy flows where my attention goes.
- I remember to be in conscious awareness of my thoughts.
- I remember to check in with my body that is affected by my "thoughts".
- I remember to pay attention to my thought patterns and focus on what I want instead of what I don't want.

Happy Mindful Meditation #7
1-Minute Smile

How you think and how you feel creates a state of BEing. Smiling can be a wonderful way to change the way you think and the way you feel. When you practice moving into an elevated state with your mind and heart, you are creating a sense of coherence and a state of well-being. It's a great exercise. I challenged my granddaughter to hold a smile for 5 whole minutes when she was being a bit pouty. It worked. Her attitude and mood changed, and we all got a good laugh around it. I hope you enjoy your happy mindful moment.

- Find a quiet comfortable place, ensuring yourself that your time and space are regarded without interruption.
- Sit comfortably and begin being conscious of your breathing. Just focus on your breath, inhaling and exhaling, noticing how you take in air and how you release air.
- With your eyes open, let yourself smile for no good reason.
- Hold the smile for about a minute or two.
- Feel your cheeks tighten and your mouth widen.
- Be aware of what happens in your facial muscles.
- When you look around, let your eyes smile too.
- See everything through your smile.
- Take a nice deep breath and thank yourself for giving yourself the time.

Going Inward Before the Meal

How did you feel looking around the room while smiling? Did it change the way in which you saw before and after you let yourself smile? Identify one essence that came to the surface. Keep alive in your mind what essence came up for you. You are now ready to bring the energy of that essence to your cooking and the Table of Life.

Sarah's Say, "Cheeeeeeeeese" Platter

My daughter, Sarah is the Queen of Cheese Platters. I love how she puts these works of art together, and we share ideas. It's fun! Sarah says, "I typically buy most of my ingredients from Trader Joe's, but often buy cheeses from various places." She takes cheese platter making as an art form. ENJOY! Pair it with your favorite wine.

Serves 8-10
Prep time: 35 minutes

Ingredients

Dried Fruit: **Persimmons, Apricots, Dates (flavored or regular pieces), Apple Rings, Dried Cherries**

Fresh Fruit: **Thinly Sliced Apples, Thinly Sliced Pears, Thinly Sliced Peaches, Persimmon (if in season), Grapes (green & red), Lychees (if in season)**

Nuts: **Marcona Almonds (Flavored - Truffle or Rosemary flavored) or Regular, Salted Cashew Pieces, Sweet Flavored Pecans**

Herbs: **(mostly for decoration and totally optional): Rosemary or Mint Leaves**

Spreads/Jams: **Fruit Pepper Jelly, Apple Butter (or pumpkin or persimmon butter), Apricot Jelly**

Cheeses: **Drunken Goat, Manchego, Port Salut, Brie, Ewephoria, Goat cheese log (regular, honey flavored, fruit flavored, or garlic flavored), Sharp Cheddar block, Havarti Dill, Cheddar with onion, Cheese with Truffles, Mini Mozzarella Balls, Asiago/Parmesan block, Beemster. Blue Cheese is the only one that you'll never see on my Cheese Platters. That particular pungent smell doesn't sit well with me.**

Crackers: **Different shapes and sizes is the key. Some long cracker sticks, round water crackers, gluten free rounds, flavored crackers, such as beet crackers (they are dark red, so that brings in a nice color to the plate), square crackers with raisins or different seeds, long rectangular garlic crackers.**

(The Method is continued on the next page)

Method

I asked Sarah to share with us how she approaches making her cheese platters. In Sarah's words: "The most important thing for me, as I am preparing a cheese platter is to visualize how the end product is going to look like. I like to use different sizes, shapes, colors, and tastes for my boards, to make them look alive and colorful.

I usually start by placing the blocks of cheeses on the platter. Depending on the size of the platter you are using, I try to have at least 3-10 options of cheese.

Regardless of your type of platter, make sure to spread your cheeses out. It is nice to have smaller pieces of cheese as well, not just blocks. I often cut or start the block with several smaller pieces of cheese and lay them on the platter in a waterfall-like pattern. Sometimes I will cut half of a block into pieces and rest those pieces against the remaining block that was not cut. I also like to cut the pieces into different shapes as well using small cookie cutters, but that's getting fancy, so do what makes you feel comfortable.

Once I have the cheeses laid out on the platter, I start to place the remaining ingredients. I like to put my jelly/jams in little ramekins, usually two per platter, and put them close to the cheeses with a little spreader next to it. Once these are on the platter, I then pour the various nuts around the platter in little piles, keeping in mind the colors that are near each other.

Fruit, dried or fresh, tends to have the most variety of color, so I usually put those on the platter last. I like to put a mix of nuts, dried, and fresh fruit near the cheese blocks/pieces, and then will fill in the empty spaces with crackers. Be mindful of not putting crackers near wet cheeses, as they will make the crackers soggy, and no one likes soggy crackers!

Oftentimes, I will have too many things on my cheese platter by choice so I will make a separate arrangement of crackers on the side. I like to top off the cheese platters with herbs as a decoration. In addition, sometimes I will take little edible flowers and use these as decoration too.

All in all, I let the platter guide me in what to do. I love using oblong, round, or long cheese platters and change it up depending on my mood. When the platter is finished, it fills my soul with so much joy! See what I mean? This is a perfect way of preparing your platter. Have fun and enjoy!"

Going Inward After the Meal

Smiling can be contagious, and it feels good, so I'm hoping that you let yourself smile for the full minute, because why not bring a smile to your life and your life experiences? What essence did you identify in this Happy Mindful Meditation? Take a moment and write it down, along with any feelings that came up about the Deep-Dive process. Was it fun? Did you enjoy the experience? Did it alter the way you cooked? Did the food seem to be a little extra yummy?

Self-Reflections/Notes

Chapter 8
Connecting: Sharing and Caring

"Life itself is the proper binge."

-Julia Child

Connecting is such a beautiful word and concept. As humans, we have a built-in need to connect, to relish, share and care about others. It's our natural inclination that helps us continue the life of our species.

Humans have been grappling with human/spiritual topics and "mysteries" since the beginning of time. Deep diving can be simple by first understanding the small things that can make a big difference. When you enter your kitchen, you are working with gas, so to speak, on all burners. You have energy that you exude, whether it be from a desire to share your cooking, or, to nourish yourself. Either way, it's energy, regardless if it's centered and positive or, anything less than that perhaps may be afflicting you. We come equipped with a natural need for connection. Connection with oneself is of first and foremost importance.

In this chapter, I'm going to share ways you can connect with yourself and others to fill up and flavor your experiences in your life with as much delight as possible – I hope you'll find them useful.

It's obvious that we need each other to survive and thrive – no human being stands alone. Even as far back as ancient Greek times, the great philosopher Aristotle said, "Man is by nature a social animal." Scientists later proved that we are actually hard-wired to connect with others, with other ideas, with other groups and individuals, and with something larger than ourselves.[13] We are not meant to be islands in isolation. Loneliness, alienation, estrangement, isolation, and distressful environment situations are terrible states for many individuals in our society. Perhaps these have always existed, however, it's our reality today as well, exacerbated by this Covid-19 pandemic. A great number of individuals feel more isolated and more alone than ever. The reasons are many. Closed environments, misunderstandings, less peace and quiet to work or just "be", are just a few things that can make individuals feel alone even with others being home. Yet, in spite of and regardless of such situations, it doesn't change the fact that neurologically we need social connection.[14]

Nowadays we have many options to connect with others, and social media has given us great advantages and possibilities to connect. However, it's the quality, and not the quantity that matters. Paradoxically, social media often manages to isolate people even further. Snap decisions to gaslight, ghost, and instant clicks on "likes" or "followers", seem to compel individuals to evaluate their self-worth as well as popularity with remarkable importance, sometimes on the basis of one photo or post. We all know that genuine, deeper connection with others can be a significant essence that can promote a better health state and well-being. I like focusing on the deeper connections that are genuine and meaningful - as these are the only ones that have the power to bring us connection with others as much as with ourselves in that equation. What promotes those deeper connections with that special element of unconditional acceptance? Let's consider pets for a moment.

---

[13] https://www.scientificamerican.com/article/why-we-are-wired-to-connect/

[14] https://dana.org/article/in-sync-how-humans-are-hard-wired-for-social-relationships/
#:~:text=%E2%80%9CHuman%20beings%20are%20wired%20to,social%20brain%20at%20the%20conference.

The desire for connection exists within animals as well. Particularly our pets like feeling in a "pack" with other similar animal breeds. Dogs are an example that quickly come to mind. Domesticated breeds snuggle up with you, you pet them with love and affection, and they feel happy as much as you do in giving them love. It's part of our evolutionary roots. Throughout the development of civilization, dogs, for example, were meant to work in different aspects on the farm, with not much regard from many farmers to how they felt or what they ate.

Later, as civilization and social advancements took place, we began to adopt them as pets, and treat them almost as humans with care, love, affection and feed them healthy nourishment. We give them unconditional love and they give it back to us in countless ways.

In giving, we are many times nourished when we feel supported by our friends, and/or families, and even a casual connection with a random stranger can award us with those happier and connected feelings. Sadly, though, there are many individuals who don't care too much what they eat since they're alone and always thinking in terms of "single portions". Eating alone is not optimally healthy for any of us humans. Repetitive frequencies of eating alone can trigger Metabolic Syndromes such as high blood pressure, cholesterol spikes, and even pre-diabetes. It also triggers an unhealthy diet, not to mention stress. During this pandemic many of us are eating alone, I know I am. Do the very best you can to make your meals as enjoyable as possible. BE creative. Let yourself feel connected and positively supported.

Connections are felt in the heart, and even though you haven't spoken to an old friend in years, as soon as you get to speak with him/her it leaves you with a feeling as if you just spoke yesterday. Love is always there – this is the essence of connection.   When love grows within you, it keeps growing, expanding, and overflows onto others.   Love never dies. We bring our essences of acceptance of ourselves, and each other with the ingredients of forgiveness, compassion, and unconditional love to the Table of Life. It starts in our kitchen.

Connecting within ourselves, as well as our higher, spiritual/soul self, means feeling connected to our body, mind and spirit as in "perfect" harmony. This is how we stay grounded, centered, ready to "take on" the world. When we feel a sense of coherence within, we are able to give of ourselves from a connected place and we feel part of something bigger than just ourselves. We feel part of, and even as one, with the world in this vast universe. The universe is part of all of us, and we are all part of it. It cannot be any other way, because ALL of it is ENERGY and that's what we are made up of… pure energy.

The beauty about knowing that we are part of a grander energy force transcends time and space, much in the same way as love does. Did you know that when we feel love, our hearts are actually expanding, filling with a vibrant blood flow?[15] When we feel connected, we feel that life force flowing within us without limiting thoughts getting in the way. We enjoy eating more, and even preparing our food and eating it with delicious focus on each delectable morsel, minus the distraction of a TV or earphones. When we feel connected with ourselves everything seems possible. When we're not, nothing seems possible, and we don't even enjoy much of anything – especially food. It's a pretty dim disconnected existence, and we feel alone as if no one understands how we feel.

A Deep-Dive connection with yourself can lead to making the decision to just pick yourself up by the bootstraps to take a good, conscious look at the condition in which you are actually living your daily life. This becomes the moment that you also

---

[15] https://www.heartmath.org/research/science-of-the-heart/energetic-communication/

become aware and examine honestly what you are bringing to the table of your life. After all, we are responsible for our own joy factor. That's living from the inside out with us at the helm.

I don't know about you, but I've lived in that place, where I have dimmed my light for the sake of others, and I have to admit, it's not the most joyful place to live, but when I was able to observe it, and recognize it, then I could shift the way in which I looked at it. If some of you have lived there too, maybe more often than wanted, or may currently be in this position, then I'm sure you know the defeated feeling of not believing that your life could get better, that changing was just not possible. I call it the 90% doubt and the 10% hope formula, and that does not make for a good recipe right there.

In addition to Love, the whole notion of believing plays a huge role in how we live our lives. It's foundational to our existence, since we act upon what we believe. Everything in life is based on a belief. Knowing something without a doubt is also an aspect that plays a significant role in how we live our lives, (some people call that faith) because it doesn't come from the thinking mind, it comes from the *knowing* mind that is rooted in the heart, that stems from love. You just know the sun will come up in the morning without a doubt and you don't even have to think about it. When we "know" (believe with our whole heart) that everything comes from love and comes back to love, Love, along with Believing and Knowing pave the way for us to understand our Joy Factor.

As you can see there are many ways of feeling connected, and it begins with yourself. Taking the time to listen to someone else and feeling empathy is another beautiful way of feeling connected, and in return brings some lasting happiness. It can promote building lasting relationships too, and when you behave genuinely as a friend to others, you may tend to live with less stress. Helping someone out of genuine kindness, with nothing expected in return, is yet another beautiful way to connect. Perhaps even consider offering sincere gratitude to another person for even the tiniest gesture. You'll see that there's truth in what Edwin Markham said about "…whatever you send into the lives of others comes back into your own…"

Have you ever caught a stranger's eye and you found yourselves both smiling? I don't know about you, but I love those moments of feeling connected. There's an "immediate" sense of intimacy, that all is okay, that humanity continues to brew goodness. Even with our required masks on, we can still see smiling eyes.

Find daily ways to laugh and laugh so hard that you can hardly catch your breath, and your stomach hurts. There are really funny movies – some are funny, and some are hilarious. You can also find insanely funny entertainment on YouTube, watch comedians, and last but not least there's laughter yoga,[16] which is great, because it's shared, and everyone gets laughing very hard. You build a small community.

When you genuinely connect you are in the moment, allowing yourself to BE. When you are truly connecting with someone, you are not thinking about the past or the future, you are just being available to the present moment and appreciating the shared experience you are having. BEing "present" is just the best feeling ever. That's why I suggest taking the few moments to do the *Happy Mindful Meditations* to practice "being" in the moment with your breath, your imagination and your heart connected. Dive down into your essence – you have it, you were born with it, use it and share it!

---

[16] https://laughteryoga.org/

When you are being yourself in an honestly candid way, you can't help but feel connected, because feeling connected doesn't work if you are trying to be something you're not. When you are you, you are able to be open and vulnerable to share your feelings and you feel connected to yourself and others. It's simply a beautiful feeling.

When you are angry, critical or judgmental, it shuts down your ability to connect. Human connection is kind, compassionate and empathetic. We also feel connected when we feel a true sense of trust, which can even happen between strangers, allowing someone to help us by putting our groceries in the car or getting something down from a shelf.

If we are "trying" to connect with someone by "being interesting, funny or smart" we may be looking for their reactions and approval, rather than being authentic or caring. We may be more interested in what we are "getting" out of the situation than what we are "giving". And, if we think we are connecting by commiserating with someone about someone else who we dislike, that is not based on trust and true connection. It's just gossip. Gossiping with others is not truly connecting, it's just talking about someone with disrespect. "Lashon hara" means evil tongue in Hebrew. When you speak unkindly of someone, Hebrew tradition considers it worse than "murder" because you're "killing" three people, the person you're talking to, the person you're talking about, and yourself. Lashon hara can destroy lives and toxify yours.

I'm sure you can describe many wonderful connections you've had when sharing a good meal with your family and friends whom you love. Entertaining can be so much fun, and it can feel like love in abundance filling your plate and your soul.

As a child my desire was to be an entertainer and a teacher, and now that I'm grown up, I see how I do both. I just love seeing the smiles on people's faces being in good company, having delicious conversations and eating yummy food together. There's nothing more satisfying than bringing that kind of sharing and caring to the Table of Life.

Growing up in a big family, we always had big gatherings. Between my dad, his brother, and two sisters, I had ten cousins on my dad's side of the family. I loved gathering with my dad's side of the family. We always had so much fun together and all the cousins were pretty close in age. My dad and uncle shared Navy stories together and talked in double-talk sometimes… it was all fun.

My mother's side of the family was more serious. My mom had one sister and three brothers and between them I had another ten cousins, but a very different experience. My cousins were much younger than me and I actually babysat them. Going to my grandma and grandpa's house was no fun at all. We weren't allowed to do anything. Plastic covered all of the living room furniture and it was about the most unfriendly place to "play". Frankly I don't remember doing much there but eat, which at least was really good. My grandma made a banana cake that we all loved.

When I got older and became married, my sisters and I split our big gatherings and alternated at different houses. We had tons of fun together, although there was a Passover dinner where my two sisters got into a fight with mashed potatoes being thrown at each other, made worse because we had a newly emigrated Russian family who we were hosting. Embarrassing, but also part of life. These experiences help us grow. We always managed to get back to the love and always made delicious food together, and shared great times.

Having people over my house and entertaining them with good food is one of the greatest joys of living, as far as I'm concerned. I shared with you in the previous chapter that I love having people over and I always have. Hearing stories, catching up on life and sharing delicious food is a gift we can experience as a family or a group of friends. That feeling of connection is just lovely.

When my mother was 55, she had a quadruple bypass and after her recovery I threw her a surprise party in the park. 150 people showed up. We made a huge banner that said, "Ruthie Silver's Birthday Party". She walked across the park and saw these people but knew nothing about the party. She almost had another heart attack when she saw that all of these people were there for her. She felt connected to her family and friends, and we felt connected to her. We played relay races and lots of games. We had a blast. There is nothing like organizing a gala event where everyone has a great time. It's one of my favorite things to do. (You notice throughout this book I have a lot of favorite things I love). LOL.

Taking the time to make an event special means that you are bringing that precious love we spoke about in Chapter 5, **"Love, Love, Love".** I say, if you are going to create a dinner or an event around food for the people you love, bring it ALL to the table. Bring your joy, your love, your care and share it with everyone.

I've been known to throw several parties/events in my life, holding the space to be the BEST party ever! Before my friend Toni died, she wanted to have a Christmas party and I told her she would have the BEST CHRISTMAS PARTY EVER! About 250 people showed up throughout the night in her beautiful home, where people gathered around her, playing her beautiful baby grand piano, singing show tunes and songs that she and her husband Gene wrote. It was truly a testament of her life. Everyone who had experienced the years of joy and creativity with Toni and Gene felt connected to an era and we were all part of it. We all knew it would be her last Christmas party and she was soooooo happy. Everyone got a chance to say goodbye in the most loving way. Hint: when someone tells you what they want, GIVE IT TO THEM in the way THEY want it, not the way you want it. That is honoring the person in the most exquisite way.

Bite Size Re-*Minders* to Living a Yummy Delicious Life

- I remember to bring the importance of connecting with myself first, in order to build or rekindle that true connection between my human and my soul.
- I remember to bring love, joy and fun to whatever I do.
- I remember that if I am "trying" to connect with someone by "being interesting, funny or smart," I am looking for other people's reactions, rather than authentically sharing or caring.
- I remember to bring a kind word to someone, and in talking about others. Gossiping with others is not truly connecting, it's just talking about someone with disrespect.
- I remember when I do something for someone, I do out of sincerity, with no expectations, guilt or obligation.

Happy Mindful Meditation #8
Filling Your Heart with Someone You Love

Feeling connected is a basic human need. We want to feel we "belong" somewhere in our lives, whether that is in our own family, in a relationship, with a group of friends, a spiritual group, or in a class with "like-minded individuals". When we feel connected to something bigger than ourselves, we feel connected to a community or a group of people sharing the same values we have. We feel connected to our family and friends.

Sharing our lives with others is a great gift. It's a give and receive relationship. When we focus on caring about others, it's a way of being of service, raising our consciousness to a higher level of BEing. When we allow ourselves to receive, it closes the cycle of giving and receiving. We can't have one without the other.

Being in the middle of a pandemic with Covid-19 running rampant, it's challenging to connect with others without being able to physically be with each other. We need to be creative in ways we may not have thought of before. This *Happy Mindful Meditation* allows you to hold someone in your heart and feel them in your presence, allowing the love you feel to expand out to others. Enjoy the moments you give yourself. I hope you enjoy your mindful moment.

- Find a quiet comfortable place, ensuring yourself that your time and space are regarded without interruption.
- Sit comfortably and begin being conscious of your breathing. Just focus on your breath, inhaling and exhaling, noticing how you take in air and how you release air.
- Think of someone you love.
- Hold this person in your heart.
- See them smiling at you.
- Let the love you have for that person expand in your heart and send them back the love you feel.
- Sit with that juicy love.
- Feel it with all your heart and soul.
- Now, consciously send this love out to your family and friends, as it expands outward.
- Bask in the love.
- Thank yourself for giving yourself this moment.

Going Inward Before the Meal

What gift did you receive in filling your heart up with love and expanding it out? Identify one essence that came to the surface. Keep alive in your mind what essence came up for you. You are now ready to bring the energy of that essence to your cooking and to the Table of Life.

Sima's Summer Super-Food Salad

My dear beautiful friend, Sima, is a celebrity fitness and lifestyle coach, inspiring people to be the best they can be, starting with food and exercise. She inspired this recipe and it's so simple to make. Eat a healthy salad with whatever you conjure up and you will feel like you just gave yourself a gift! ENJOY!

Serves 4
Prep time: 20 minutes

Ingredients

2-3 bunches of kale, chopped (remove the stems)

1 small bag fresh baby spinach

4-6 radishes or watermelon radishes

16 Heirloom baby tomatoes)

¼ cup red onion, diced

4 Tbs toasted sunflower seeds

½ cup shredded carrots

½ cup dried cranberries

½ cup Kumquats, cut in half

Dressing:

8 Tbs raw tahini

½ squeezed lemon

1 Tbs grapeseed oil

Pinch of Sea Salt

1 clove of garlic minced

1 Tbs water

1 tsp manuka honey

1 tsp apple cider vinegar

Method

For the dressing: In a small bowl, mix all ingredients together

Add water slowly to desired consistency

For the salad: In a large bowl, mix all fresh ingredients and add the dressing. Toss until dressing is thoroughly mixed in.

Enjoy!

Going Inward After the Meal

Letting yourself feel love is very special. In this Happy Mindful Meditation, you allowed yourself to think about someone you love, and it could even have been a pet. This process was meant to bring about a sense of love in your heart and allowing it to expand out. Write down what this experience was like. How was it to let yourself feel this love and share it? How did the essence you identified permeate your cooking experience? What was the result? Any comments from family and friends?

Self-Reflections/Notes

Chapter 9
A New Way of BEing

"When a man's stomach is full it makes no difference

whether he is rich or poor."

- Euripides

Euripides was an insightful tragedian of ancient Greece. One of his contemporaries, Socrates, was a Greek philosopher from Athens. Both these men advanced the founding of a philosophy that was adopted and expanded with time in our Western world. Euripides demonstrated elements in his plays which have become imbedded in Western philosophy. Socrates is the one who is credited as being the first moral philosopher of the Western ethical tradition of thought. Truth is Truth. Love is Love. Thousands of years later, we still use Socrates' same analogy for life.

When you consciously make the decision to adopt a new way of BEing, you stifle out the old patterns that no longer serve you, and eventually you grow out of them. You eventually grow into who you want to BE consistently, living a more fulfilled, meaningful and joyful life.

When your heart is full of gratitude, appreciation, love, kindness (and all the goodies that go along with those nutritious ingredients), it makes no difference whether you are rich or poor, because you feel satiated and are able to bring a juicy sense of well-being. It comes down to emotional well-being and maintaining stability in this new way of BEing. How do you do it? Then how do you bring that essence to The Table of Life?

Start by falling in love with your imagination. Allow yourself to dive in, explore, and play in the deep end of your essences. Your imagination is your greatest gift you have been given by the Universe/Life Force/God/Love/All That Is. Imagination is your internal freedom to enjoy and see unlimited possibilities.

You use your imagination to focus on who you want to BE – to envision yourself, as well as envisioning yourself achieving what you want. The point is you really get to FEEL as if it has already happened, before it actually happens. It's signaling new genes in new ways, who seem to then come together and conspire with the Universe to create that reality, liberating the energy. [17] It's called joy. If you imagine hard enough, constantly enough, with all the details of the energy of your being in that equation, you can achieve it. The reality of it may come gently without you even sometimes being conscious of it. It's almost like waking up to a new day!

The imagination process is like a re-wire of your brain, thus secreting different chemicals that allow energy space for you to practice a new way of BEing. Over time, the new wiring continues to signal the brain with the new thoughts/images and the neural pathways form new loops that become the "new norm", ones that inspire, that feel good, that change the way in which you feel.

It's quite exciting actually, to meditate and focus on something you want, using your imagination to "see" it and the body to "feel" it. It's a team effort. Remember we talked about thoughts being the language of the mind and emotions being the language of the body in Chapter 7, **Change Your Thoughts, Change Your Life**? Well this is where it kicks in. The mind and the body work together as a team

---

[17] https://blog.drjoedispenza.com/blog/mastery-es/when-you-stop-looking-and-start-becoming

to give you the human sensation you desire. Then the energy of those thoughts and images go "out" to the Universe and come back, and watch out, something wonderful will happen in an unexpected and surprising way!

I think we can agree that our bodies change according to our thoughts. Using your imagination, you can "see" the experience you want, "as if it has already happened" in the quantum energy field of the Universe. Then, when you let yourself FEEL the experience, your body registers the feelings as if the experience has already happened, because remember, the mind doesn't differentiate between it being real or not, and allows the Universe to give you experiences in the way you least expect, catching you off guard, leaving no doubt that there is a greater reality than being in a body and it makes it all that much more delicious.

When we live by the hormones of stress and survival, we want to control the outcome. When we move into the state of creation, we're moving into the heart and in love with our imagination. Haven't you ever noticed that sometimes we place more credence on the "worst case scenario" than we do a "great one"? Why is doubting that something wonderful can happen easier than believing something wonderful can happen? Who knows why we don't allow ourselves to fully feel the sensation of having a wonderful experience, even if it is not happening right now? Who cares?

Just letting yourself HAVE the experience in the first place is worth it, even if it never manifests. Many times, I envision something really fun happening, and I can actually FEEL the experience in every fiber of my being. I feel excited, jazzed, pumped up and that feeling carries me for a long time. I can see it, feel it and experience it as if it is already happening. My body doesn't know the difference, so I just go with it. I see myself as a New York Times Best Selling Author. I get so excited just thinking about it. If I died in the next moment and that didn't happen, it wouldn't matter, because I gave myself the experience of having it in my mind and my body got the benefit.

We can also have that experience by living vicariously through others. As a little girl I wanted to be a child star, like Shirley Temple. I watched Ted Mack's Amateur Hour and wanted to act and sing and entertain. When Bette Midler came along, watching her sing and act was so satisfying and just watching her do it was enough. I imagined I was her and every time I saw her, I felt excited, as if that was me living vicariously through her.

I know it may all sound simple, but many times, when we have an enjoyable experience, we tend to minimize or dismiss it as, "just an experience" and we "throw it away" rather than allowing the experience to sink in to reprogram the brain. We need to savor this state of BEing, rather than discard it as "nothing".

When we minimize a positive experience we are having, we negate the joy factor in the experience and diminish the importance of having it matter. When we consciously "let ourselves" have an enjoyable experience, we are training our brains to wire neurologically that positive experience and we experience an "elevated emotion". The more we help the positive experiences sink into our body, the more the negative neural pathways become "replaced" by the positive experiences. What's important is to let the experience "in", feeling it in every part of your being, even in the places that feel unloved when you were a child, allowing it to sink into those places inside where you felt not enough. Once you let it seep into your beingness, then you can detach and let it go in a healthy way, like a beautiful butterfly.

As adults, we have the ability to choose our states of BEing. When we are attached to the past, especially the negative experiences, we sometimes hold onto those memories more readily than the positive experiences and they not only affect our present but infringe on our future. Remember, we are wired for impending danger, so it makes sense, but we are also wired for love, so that opens up all the endless possibilities.

As children we usually allow more positive experiences to occur naturally and more easily, until all the "no's and don'ts" come in, so we have to spend some time unlearning what we don't want to consume. We then rewire our brains for the experiences we would rather eat and digest. Remember that everything we do in life begins internally and we are the CEO of our own lives. We are responsible for what we bring to our lives. There are steps you can take to practice allowing yourself to restore your emotional sense of well-being and stability.

Start with letting yourself HAVE a positive experience, letting the good feeling enter your body, feeling relaxed, present, and energized. Sometimes people feel unworthy or undeserving to feel joy, so they don't let themselves experience it at all. It's important to overstep that "feeling" of unworthiness and let yourself feel the sense of well-being in different parts of your body.

Once you have activated any positive experience you want to have, allow it to marinate there for few a seconds or so, bringing an intensity and intention to the equation. BEing conscious of sitting up straight or putting your hand on your heart helps you to stay present with the positive experience you want to have. This is enriching your experience, like stirring the cream from the top into the body of the ingredients, letting the experience saturate into every pore of your being.

The next step is to allow yourself to absorb what you are experiencing, by using your senses in priming your memory systems to become extra super-duper absorbent, so it really sinks in, like a warm cup of cocoa on a cold night, letting yourself change for the better.

When you notice something pleasant in you, pause for a moment and really experience it, inviting all the good feeling thoughts to the "party" with an ongoing sense of well-being, allowing yourself to dwell in the positive experience, and with time, this will sink into you more easily.

Let's say you want to feel cared about. Bring to mind someone that you know cares about you today or it could be in the past, or it can even be a pet or someone who has passed away. KNOWING they care about you without a doubt and allowing yourself to feel that is like lighting a fire in your heart, where you genuinely feel liked or appreciated, feel seen, included or loved. Any one of these experiences are examples of feeling cared about.

Helping this experience become more intense and getting a sense that it is sinking into you like water in a sponge, strengthens your effort and with time begins to rewire your brain, creating your inner sanctuary where you feel gratitude, joy, contentment, towards your desires, wants, goals, wishes, passions, purposes. The secret is to help yourself by learning what you want with a genuine desire.

The key is you need to be a friend to yourself, standing up for yourself, giving yourself permission to have a positive experience for at least 10 seconds in a row.

When you open your heart, you become so powerful and connected to others, it increases all the hormones that make you feel a sense of well-being and peace and love and kindness and all those ingredients that make for an abundant main course life.

When you are judgmental or angry, your system shrinks and your heart contracts. When your heart opens up, it opens up your energy field and has an effect on everybody you interact with. The key is to consciously change your thinking, and when you focus on what you want and not what you don't want, you are "remembering your future". When you focus on your past and not your future, you are "remembering your past" and creating it again and again, so the future will be the same.

It does take a lot of courage to change, and you are worth changing for. What else more important is there to "do"? Give yourself permission to take care of yourself and be kind to yourself. Be your own best friend. Remember too that when you want to change and no longer want to think the same thoughts, you are breaking the chemical continuity.

I always say, "It's your life. Enjoy the journey. And remember to bring love into everything you do." When you bring honor and reverence to yourself and others, you are bringing it to the Table of your Life.

Bite Size Re-*Minders* to Living a Yummy Delicious Life

- I remember to open my heart and be grateful.
- I remember to nurture my relationship between my imagination, my heart and soul and be my own best friend.
- I remember to fill myself up with positive experiences and let myself feel the elevated emotions.
- I remember that it's okay to imagine what I want and who I want to be and let myself HAVE the experience in the moment.
- I remember that I am worth changing my thoughts and my life for, that I deserve to live a happy, joyous life with a sense of well-being.

Happy Mindful Meditation #9
Using Your Eyes to See

Sometimes we take for granted that we are able to see, even without our physical ability to see. Our imagination is one of the greatest gifts humans have been given. We can imagine and re-imagine when we want to contemplate a different way of being. Using your imagination in a way that elevates yourself heightens and uplifts your spirit. When you become mindful of what you are seeing, your sight expands, and your vision increases. Letting yourself use your gift of sight enhances your senses.

When was the last time you examined a leaf? Did you notice its veins? Life runs through everything. This *Happy Mindful Meditation* helps you get in touch with all living things. I hope you enjoy your mindful moment.

- Find a quiet comfortable place, near a window, ensuring yourself that your time and space are regarded without interruption.
- Sit comfortably and begin being conscious of your breathing. Just focus on your breath, inhaling and exhaling, noticing how you take in air and how you release air.
- Look outside the window.
- Notice what you see.
- Find something in nature and just look at it, whether it's a tree or a plant or a bird sitting on a wire or flying by.

- Notice the colors, the shapes, the different sizes.

- Appreciate how nature gives us beauty and sustenance.

- Let yourself feel blessed by the gifts that nature gives.

Going Inward Before the Meal

What did you see out the window? Were you able to appreciate nature's gifts? Did you see things you normally don't see? Identify one essence that came to the surface. Keep alive in your mind what essence came up for you. You are now ready to bring the energy of that essence to your cooking and the Table of Life.

_____

_____

_____

_____

The Silver Girls' Caramel Praline Cheesecake

I thought I would add another sweet recipe, one that was passed down from my grandmother, and who passed it on to her, I have no idea. Someone had to make up this recipe. All I know is that it is D E L I C I O U S and my sister Judy, and my niece, Dahlia, added their instinctive creativity to it, and made it with Caramel Praline and boy, is it ever YUMMY! They use it in their gluten free Twice Baked Bakery in Long Beach, California. ENJOY!

Serves 8-10
Prep time: 30 minutes
Bake time: 35 minutes
Total time: 65 minutes

Ingredients

Filling:
3 eggs
2 8oz. cream cheese
1 cup sugar
¼ tsp salt
2 tsp vanilla extract
½ tsp almond extract**
3 cups sour cream

Crust:
1 ¾ cup cinnamon graham cracker crumbs (You can use gluten free cinnamon graham crackers if you want to make it gluten free)

¼ cup fine raw walnuts (You can omit the walnuts and almond extract if you want to make it nut free. I have to admit, it does taste wonderful with the whole shebang!)

Topping:
½ - 1 cup of pecan pralines from Trader Joes (beware, you might want to eat them before you even get them onto the cheesecake)

1 jar caramel sauce in a jar from Trader Joes

Note: When putting crust into the pan, spoon enough of this topping mixture on the top of the crust BEFORE you add the filling.

Note: Use a springform pan where the sides can be removed from the base. This will make it so much easier to take out and you'll see the beautiful bottom crust when done.

Method

Preheat the oven at 375 degrees.

Crust:

Put the cinnamon graham crackers and raw walnuts in a food processor. Check it after a couple of moments, so you don't overmix it into a grain like texture, but more of a crumble. Remove and pour into a bowl.

Add the melted butter and mix ingredients together with a fork to get it nice and crumbly.

Press the crust into a springboard pan and up the sides. Even the crust out, while patting it down, and don't be afraid if it's too thick. I'm telling you this crust is unbelievably tasty.

Take the pecan pralines and put them in the food processor (same one you used for the crust) until crumbly, but not too fine. Take a few tablespoons of pecan praline mixture and spread the mixture over the top of the crust to cover evenly.

Filling:

Take a mixing bowl and put in both 8 ounces of cream cheese packages, and 1 cup of sugar. Cream together until nice and smooth.

Add 3 eggs, one at a time, and continue to cream.

Add salt, vanilla and almond extract and mix together.

Blend in 3 cups of sour cream. Once it is nice and creamy-creamy, wipe the sides of the bowl clean, get as much of this mixture as possible

Pour it into the crust and put in the oven at 375 degrees and bake for 35 minutes or so.

Remove from oven and cool it for an hour, not in the refrigerator. Before you put it into the refrigerator, take another spoonful or so of the pecan praline mixture and put it on the top.

Take the caramel mixture and put in the microwave for about 25 seconds and drizzle it over the top. Be creative, you can make a pattern, a circle or whatever you want. Then add, if you want, a little more pecan praline on top of the caramel sauce, so when you put it into a container it won't stick to the caramel sauce.

When I have made this, I whip the cream cheese first alone, then add sugar, and then add the eggs, extracts.

Going Inward After the Meal

Being aware of nature is another way of helping us to stay present. Write down what essence came up for you, while gazing out the window, and how it impacted your cooking. Did you enjoy that process? Did you notice anything different in the way in which you cooked? Were you more present? Did it alter your approach to all aspects of the cooking experience? Was it enjoyable? Did you hear any reactions from family and friends?

Self-Reflections/Notes

_____

_____

_____

_____

_____

_____

_____

_____

_____

_____

_____

_____

_____

Chapter 10
BEing your Legacy

"I think the whole world is dying to hear someone say, 'I love you.' I think that if I can leave the legacy of love and passion in the world, then I think I've done my job in a world that's getting colder and colder by the day."

— Lionel Richie

Living a life filled with love and passion in the world is BEing and living your legacy. When boundless love, compassion, kindness is genuinely exuded from you, and spills over to your friends, family, acquaintances and even random individuals in casual conversations, then all of those individuals feel good from that loving kindness. This is what all these individuals will always remember, over and over. They will be inspired to adopt a dose of your brand of love, kindness and compassion to carry into their world, and thus bring it to the Table of Life.

Love, kindness and compassion towards others, in the most sincere and authentic sense, is a Legacy. Money is useful and can serve as a legacy too, but everyone touched by you will have that distinct memory of having been "loved" by you through kindness and compassion. We are wired to want to be loved for ourselves, but in giving is where you receive love too. Why else would we be wired to care, if not to touch someone else's life, leave something of immeasurable value behind us, as a testament for our being alive, having lived a life? If we weren't wired that way, our future generations would just cease to continue. We would all just grab what we could "get" from life, be totally self-absorbed, and not care about others or what we bring to life.

There are many people who walk the earth like this, and some have their own circumstances, no doubt, but it is very sad. It's a decision that each one has the power and the right to make to move far away from an energetic place of misery, bitterness, anger, jealousy, greed, doubt, feeling unworthy, not enough, living with limited possibilities, blame, rage, control, etc. You may know someone like this in your life and the sad part is that these negative energies are passed on to their children and even grandchildren.

The concept of legacy is a profoundly interesting one. People think of gifts such as money, real estate, cars, awards and mementos as legacies to leave to their beloved after they have passed away. However, here I am addressing the notion of BEing your legacy. BEing your legacy is passionately immersing and saturating your whole self into the life you love living, the life that embraces Your Own Uniqueness (Y.O.U). The life that you feel blessed to have, no matter what the circumstances may be, already serves to attract more of all good things into your life. Everything looks that much better when you feel blessed, and others feel that around you. It's an energy being shared in a beautiful way. It's uplifting.

Love is Energy. Energy is also the consistent ingredient in everything we are, do, say and see. That's why when we recognize what we are experiencing, and are conscious of what we do, say and see, we are the legacy that will live on. Living now with values that mean something, with that special, kindly loving demeanor that touches hearts and lifts the spirit.

Time flies by ever so quickly, especially the older we get. There is no doubt about that, especially in the scope of history, we are but a flicker, so it's how we do what we do with our lives that matters. That is our legacy. That is what we live and pass on. Everything alive dies eventually, except for energy. Remember that energy only changes form, so when this human form changes into a formless form, the energy of the human being remains, just in a different form.

Talking about a formless form, I once studied with Swami Kaleshwar in India, and he did something that was pretty phenomenal. He put himself in a state of 'Samadhi',[18] which means he separated the body from its soul, actually bringing together and unifying his mind, willing his energy to change form into a formless form (we call death). He felt that his teachings would be carried in the ether beyond his body. That is the transformation, from human to soul. We talk about soul to human, but it is both ways.

A human being's life journey can be compared with a butterfly's life, valuable, fleeting, and beautiful. Even though we may wish a butterfly could stay longer to appreciate its beauty, we still feel a sense of awe just to have been able to see it in that brief, transitory moment. In the same regard, when we share an encounter with a fellow human being, we are left with something from them, as they are left with something from us, just by our existence. We come into each other's lives for a reason. We touch each other in time and space, engaging in delicious life experiences, stirring them into a beautiful work of art. When someone touches a butterfly, they will often lose scales that could prevent them from flying. These scales strengthen and stabilize their wings. In humans, we often let people touch us, and hold us back from the very things we are meant to do; fly and be free.

----

[18] https://en.wikipedia.org/wiki/Samadhi

As I mentioned above, if you look at living as a blessing, you are blessed to be in your body for however long you get to experience being you. It's just as precious as a butterfly's life. Your existence is of great value. Those values are passed on each moment you are living and transform after you die. Your life's journey is full of rich impactful moments, and these moments of enlightenment and learning are founded in your growth of wisdom, creating noteworthy experiences filled with precious nuggets of anecdotal understandings and life reflections as your legacy to family and friends. Therefore, you must first believe in your own self-worth and know that your presence is of utmost value. You are the gift, and Nature is a great teacher of life. We get to live out the cycle of hundreds of millions of inhales and exhales, life and death, and everything in between, and beyond.

When you feel that you are living your idea of a meaningful, fun, joyful and blessed life, then you are able to contribute to the world, (*big or small*) as a beautiful cycle of giving and receiving, so that your gift of *BEing* will be given to all whom you touch, reaching life beyond your own, outliving and outlasting your time on earth. As mentioned before, love transcends time and space. All those who will have been touched by your love, will be so enriched with their own, and just imagine what they bring to the Table of Life. Therefore, expressing your love and sharing it with others, while you are living is a way of leaving love behind wherever you go, like little crumbs that Hansel and Gretel left behind them to find their way back home.

Our desire to live, love and be loved is very high. I really enjoy everything I do in life. I think that's the deep joy we get to feel, along with that wonderful, can't live without it, sense of well-being. I'll have many doses of well-being, thank you very much.

Your ancestors' life lessons and recipes passed onto you from your parents and grandparents are another form of legacy they passed on to you, given from generation to generation, and your life lessons and recipes are your legacy that you pass on and share with your children and grandchildren. You are leaving a legacy behind that is irreplaceable. Your positivity and thirst for constant learning, is something your kids will have forever.

Lifelong legacies are a string of single moments that make up one whole life, like a string of pearls, each one offering a whole experience. Sometimes BEing your own living legacy requires you to step outside yourself and give your entire heart for one moment to something you care about. Never underestimate the power of your actions. With one small gesture you can change a person's life for the better. We cross paths with other people's lives for a reason – hardly anything is random or coincidental. Think about legacy as a series of small gestures you can make on a daily basis. It always starts with you being you, authentically, lovingly, sincerely, happily, joyfully, and gratefully.

It is wise to never underestimate the smallest gesture of kindness. A kind word, a sweetly casual smile, a post-it note with a sweet message, being present, listening to another person, holding space without judgment is a huge gift that will carry on ahead as a legacy. When you "are" as you are, you are modeling a legacy of living. There is nothing ordinary about having walked the earth, having a purpose with passion, serving to inspire, even for five minutes. Maybe you don't really know how you've impacted someone's life. Maybe you will come to realize at one point in your life that you did have an impact along the road of life, and so age may allow you to see life from a different perspective.

When we do not feel our own sense of self-worth, we diminish the feeling for the possible impact we may have on others. Sometimes we feel we're not "enough" because of emotional type circumstances that have worn away some self-esteem. However, even in such a case, we are able to hear someone, listen to them and offer consolation and hope. This too, however, you may deem as tiny, but actually ends up giving that individual renewed belief in life. One life at a time. Not everyone is made to save "millions" of lives and souls at a time like Gandhi, Nelson Mandela, or Mother Teresa. We cannot compare ourselves to others. If we do, we reduce our sense of worth and value, questioning what we might have to offer the world.

Flowers don't have to "do" anything to be beautiful. Trees are still and stay in one place for a very long time and they provide shade, and even food.[19] Butterflies don't have to "do" anything to be appreciated for their beauty. They are themselves and spread pollen from one flower to another for us to admire their beauty. They just "are".

Living *your* particular life journey is unique, not only in the way you perceive the world, but in the way in which you express what your experiences are. Capturing your essence can be vital in feeling worthy, realizing you make a difference, just by being you. My friend Toni was always so wise and insightful. She always used to say, "In a million other galaxies, on a thousand other stars, there will never, ever be another you!"

When my dad was dying, he expressed remorse, feeling like a failure as a father, a husband and provider. I wanted him to see that his life mattered, that he was instrumental in making all of us who we are, that WE were his living legacy. My sister in law and I created a montage video of his life with tons of photos of his family and friends surrounding him, along with his favorite music so he could see his life had value, as he was dying. We played that video over and over and over and you know what happened? Dad died with a smile on his face, feeling blessed and loved up. What a way to go! It just goes to show that it's never too late to change the way you think and feel... even up to your very last breath!

In reading the various Chapters in this book, I do hope that you've been inspired to Deep-Dive, contemplate your life, recognize the true value of your unique self, and the power that is within you to affect others in the most positive ways. Remember that we are all part of that bigger Energy system – the Life Force and Land of Infinite Possibilities, with shared qualities from which we learn and admire.

Whether you are retired, inspired, at peace, at the beginning or end of life, wherever you are, relating your life experience in a naturally flowing way, without any bitterness or resentment, is a gift. The question is, how do you determine your value and growth through day to day "ordinary" things? How do you extract meaning and importance from doing what you perceive as, "nothing" in your life? You can begin by sharing some anecdotal examples from your day to day life experiences.

Here are a few examples of what you can focus on:
- What are you thankful for?
- Who are you thankful for?
- Who are people in your life that have thanked you for something you did? (*No example is too small.*)
- What did you do to help someone else? (*Don't take this part for granted. It may have been something you think was small, but to the person you helped, it made all the difference in the world.*)

* Who do you love?

Remember that everyone you come into contact with, has been impacted and touched by your life existence. Maybe you came from an abusive background, or maybe you came from a tough neighborhood. Your resilience and how you came to live the life you love in spite of that is inspiring. The journey of how you came to a place in your life where you carry a sense of well-being and joy, are even noteworthy essentials for a memoir. Don't underestimate the value of your life experiences. Someone somewhere will learn something from your pearls of wisdom.

When you share your truth, other people can perhaps identify with a truth in their own life. Truth is truth with transferrable universal principles which are timeless, transcending cultures, religions, genders and age. Who can argue with kindness, fairness, justice, respect, honesty, integrity and service?

As humans, it is easy to see the dynamic between what we think and feel, judging our self-worth, and believing that we have little value that actually makes an impact on other people's lives. The value that doing the small "nothings" in life means more than you think. Your life matters. You make a difference just by being alive. You impact others with your actions, words and deeds! You leave your mark upon the hearts of those you touch. Just as a butterfly, you are unique and beautiful in your own unique and beautiful way and your being has value. This is your living legacy.

Bite Size Re-*Minders* to Living a Yummy Delicious Life

- I remember that a human being's life journey is very much like a butterfly's life, valuable, fleeting, and beautiful.

- I remember to believe in my own self-worth and know that my presence is of utmost value and cannot compare myself to others.

- I remember I have an effect on others, no matter how "minor" I think it is, it has long lasting effects, whether I am conscious of it or not.

- I remember I am a one-of-a-kind unique human being and have my own gifts to give to others.

- I remember that I am a living legacy.

Happy Mindful Meditation #10
Becoming No-Body in Space

We may know intellectually that we are leaving a legacy of who we are behind us. However, being in a body, we can sometimes feel limited, because we appear to be solid matter. When we allow ourselves to go beyond our limitations, we begin to expand our awareness and realize that we are more than a body, that we are ultimately connected to the vast Universe.

Remember that every atom is 99.999999% space and that there is space that exists between every part of your body, including your organs, your bones, your blood, your muscles, etc. This *Happy Mindful Meditation* allows you to have the sensation of so much space, you become "no body". Going into space, you become just waves and particles. I hope you enjoy your mindful moment.

- Find a quiet comfortable place, ensuring yourself that your time and space are regarded without interruption.
- Sit comfortably and begin being conscious of your breathing. Just focus on your breath, inhaling and exhaling, noticing how you take in air and how you release air.
- Gently close your eyes.
- Take a nice deep belly breath, filling yourself up with your own life force and exhale any tension that might be lingering.

- Keep your focus on your breathing effortlessly inhaling and exhaling.

- Now, for a moment, imagine the space that exists between your eyes.

- Now imagine this space in space.

- Feel your body disappear as a teeny tiny spec in this limitless space, breathing and letting your body become waves and particles of the universe.

- Take a few more breaths and bring your awareness back into the room, back into your body, right here and now, feeling totally refreshed and ready to greet your next experience.

Going Inward Before the Meal

What did it feel like to let yourself go inside to become aware of the space that exists between your eyes? What was the sensation you felt when you let yourself float into space and become "one" with the universal space that exists? Identify one essence that came to the surface. Keep alive in your mind what essence came up for you. You are now ready to bring the energy of that essence to your cooking and the Table of Life.

Jake's Fav Chocolate Chip Banana Muffins

My grandson, Jake, LOVES chocolate, and so I always add chocolate chips to this recipe that was passed down to me from the Whizin side of the family. It's a fail proof recipe that always comes out great. Just don't leave the muffins in too long. They are much better when a little moist. I've also made them with butterscotch chips. Those were yummy too! ENJOY!

Serves 12
Prep time: 20 minutes
Bake time: 20-25 minutes
Total time: 40-45 minutes

Ingredients

¾ cup sugar

½ cups room temperature butter

2 eggs, room temperature

1 tsp baking soda

4 generous Tbs sour cream

1 cup mashed bananas

1 ½ cups pastry flour

¼ tsp salt

1 tsp vanilla extract

¼ - ½ cups mini chocolate chips

Method

Preheat oven to 350º F.
Dissolve soda in sour cream, set aside, let soda bubble up.
Cream butter & sugar.
Add eggs then beat lightly.
Add sour cream & soda and add to egg mix.
Add bananas alternately with flour, salt & vanilla.
Mix slightly then add chocolate chips.
Spray muffin tins with nonstick olive oil. I like the crispy outer layer.
Bake in muffin pans for 20-25 minutes.
Check on the muffins

Lemon Icing (optional)

1 cup powdered sugar

1 tablespoon lemon

1 tablespoon boiling water

Optional: Place lemon juice and water in a bowl.
Place lemon juice and water in a bowl.
Add sugar until mixture is thick enough to spread.

Notes

Muffins come out a little too dry if I wait for a knife to come out cleanly. Better to leave it too moist.

Going Inward After the Meal

Space is a large subject and allowing yourself to go into space can be quite fun. In becoming more of the universal energy and less physical, how did that impact your experience in cooking? Were you lighter, freer? Did it alter the way in which you approached cooking? Write down what you experienced, if it was enjoyable and some other essences that may have popped up.

Self-Reflections/Notes

Chapter 11
Contributing to the World

"I have found that among its other benefits, giving liberates the soul of the giver."

-Maya Angelou

When you go shopping for food, think of all the people you help contribute to their livelihood as well, just by buying fresh vegetables or any other food product. The farmers, the pickers, the packers, the truck drivers, the distributors, the stores' employees, your family, your friends, and many, many others are impacted by shopping. Every time you buy anything, whether it's food, fruit, or household goods, you are contributing to someone's life in this world. Somebody has to make, grow, pick, pack and deliver something you eat, drink, touch, wear, sleep on, sit on, or walk on. Every person contributes to us by making everything we use, and we contribute to them by buying it and using whatever they make or produce.

Now consider how you honor what they bring. How do you then cook the food? Are you hurried, stressed, and make "short cuts" out of boredom? Growth requires patience and good consistent care. It's good to be present in your essence when you cook. Understand that you're honoring yourself, and it takes focused practice to be patient and give good consistent care to each step of what you're making. Focus on how easy it was to bring all the different ingredients home without you having you to grow, care and harvest every single thing. This is a good moment to give gratitude for having obtained these so easily. There are so many ways of contributing to the world. Gratitude is only one as it sends out boundless good energy. It can only attract more of the same too. It's best when you speak it and share it with others. They learn from your gratitude and soon emulate it as well. Friends and family will always remember they "learned" it from you. That's instant legacy too, and it goes hand in hand with contributing to the world!

When we love and care for others, we are contributing to the world. Some contributions are one-on-one, while others are to a group of people. Regardless, even one person touched by genuine love by you can go on to grow a village. When we are kind, and thoughtful and genuinely interested in others, we are contributing to the world. We are thus leaving a legacy of having loved and been kind as much as possible, with no intent to harm or damage. This conscious living is the very essence of what you "bring" to the Table of Life. It's an awareness of the essences that YOU bring to the Table, to live a delicious life.

Love breeds more love and it's the gift that keeps on giving, so whenever you give of your true self with love, you are contributing to the world and multiplying the essence. It's your legacy and each one's is unique.

Not everyone, however, is inclined to contribute to the world, or care about a "legacy". That's ok – to each their own. Some people seem to not particularly care about having a belief system regarding contributing to the world. They're fine with just going along in life neutrally. These people may also think that they have nothing to give or offer that would be of value to the world. This is why it's so important to connect with your essence – you may discover hidden treasures about yourself.

When you authentically have a desire to give to others, that desire comes from a place of inner joy. I truly believe that when you bring honor, dignity, regard, and love to what you do, say, and share, then life couldn't be anything other than joyful, honorable, and loving.

Sometimes, when you are obsessing about your own problems or are stuck in a "feeling bad" loop, focusing on someone else's needs is a way to uplift you out of your feelings. It's also a beautiful act of kindness, because you are supporting their life. Your support helps them make their life better, and that cycle goes around and around. When you give and contribute from the heart and someone benefits from the contribution in any way, that's the reward. It's a giving/receiving cycle that comes full circle. It's in the giving that the receiving takes place, not in the expectation of getting.

One small gesture to another human being may seem like a small gesture to you but could be a humongous gesture to that person. Just calling someone you love is a way of genuinely touching someone. It lets them know you think of them and you care.

Be a good listener. There is nothing more honorable and respectful than being genuinely interested in another human being. There is great value in feeling heard by someone who really cares.

Contributing to the world starts in your heart. When you recognize that you have a purpose in your life, which can be as simple as giving and receiving love, you get to feel a sense of fulfillment and gratitude.

In the Jewish tradition, it is said that healing one person is like healing the world. Giving doesn't have to be so "grand" that it feels unattainable. It is also important to bring compassion when you contribute to the world, and not berate, shame or humiliate anyone for being in the situation they are in.

Giving your time is a huge way to contribute to the world. Time is the greatest gift we can give another. Do you have someone in your life who is elderly and could use some company? Well, it may be a bit challenging right now with this pandemic, but many would welcome a call.

You can also contribute to others by having a sense of humor through bringing a bit of laughter and smiles to them, especially now as we face adversity. It doesn't take much.

Create and hold a vision for your life's journey and how you want to BE engaged with your life. See how your Joy Factor and your passion become contagious, inspiring others to reconnect with something deeper inside themselves as well.

When I was 19, my friend, Regina and I, hitchhiked across Europe for 6 months and then decided to go to Israel. On the flight there, I became overwhelmingly excited with the idea of visiting the land of my historical ancestors. I was highly idealistic, and I became inspired to contribute something to the country. It occurred to me to enter the army.

We arrived in Israel and we went straight to a kibbutz office the very next day. Israel was made up of different kibbutzim (communes), some agricultural, some industrial, all based on a community approach sharing the responsibilities of the kibbutz. The agent was describing the different kinds of kibbutzim they had, and I wanted to go where I was "needed". Would you imagine that we had some gall to ask *if they had a kibbutz with a swimming pool?*

The agent brought out a huge 12"x18" hard, leather-bound book, opened it up, flipped through the pages, and with her fingers, went down the entire list, suddenly stopping and saying, "Oh, here's a kibbutz with a swimming pool, that desperately needs girl volunteers." Well, that did it for me! Then, she said, "but it is on the Jordanian border and there may be bombing." At first, I thought, "Oh crap!" I had never ever been around bombs. I couldn't let my parents know I was in the Jordan Valley.

Then, I heard myself saying, "I'll go, I'll serve. I want to go where I'm needed. I want to contribute to my people." And so, it was, and that's what my friend and I did. The rest of this story is *something else*, and I'll save that for another time, but my point is that I became inspired to contribute, and we had no expectation of any reward, or pats on the back.

When you give of yourself make the contribution heartfelt, from a place of love for all. Let your hands be genuine in the giving and your words encouraging in their sound. Give from the inside out and welcome the outside in.

Here's a mantra that can serve to remind you, "…one person may not change the world, but they may change the world for one person." It only takes one for the ripples to spread. Be that person. You can make this world a better place.

I hope that something I've said in this book resonates with something in you to inspire you, uplift you, and makes your life better, from good to GREAT.

Repairing the world (*Tikkun Olam*) is a concept taken from the ancient Judaic tradition. It's in your power to now make a decision to be consciously aware of who and how you are right now. The path to knowing what you "bring" to the Table of life and to the world will become clear.

Bite Size Re-*Minders* for Living a Yummy Delicious Life

- I remember that coming from the heart, with love and care for others is a way of contributing to the world. My existence can become my own legacy.

- I remember to be kind, thoughtful and genuinely interested in others, as a way of contributing to the world.

- I remember to be conscious of what I bring to the Table of Life, whether volunteering my skills, my talents or my time, that I am contributing to the world.

- I remember that even in the small gestures, I am contributing to the world.

- I remember it's in the giving that the receiving takes place, not in the expectation of getting.

Happy Mindful Meditation #11
Smelling Your Way to BEing Present

Smelling is another one of our wonderful senses that helps us to be present. Being able to smell is a marvelous gift that works as your internal guidance system helping you enjoy life, stimulating the olfactory system delighting in the aromas of your favorite foods or the fragrance of your favorite flowers. Your sense of smell can also warn you of impending danger from gas leaks to spoiled food. Never underestimate the power of being able to smell. It also helps you taste your food. Even chewing food stimulates the olfactory system, working together with your sense of taste.

This Happy Mindful Meditation helps you get in touch with your sense of smell, allowing your olfactory system to be stimulated in an enjoyable way. I hope you enjoy your mindful moment.

- Find a quiet comfortable place, ensuring yourself that your time and space are regarded without interruption.

- Sit comfortably and begin being conscious of your breathing. Just focus on your breath, inhaling and exhaling, noticing how you take in air and how you release air.

- Pick an item that you LOVE to smell. It could be an orange, or cinnamon or a fragrant flower that you have handy.

- Gently close your eyes.

- Bring the item to your nose and breathe it in. If you are smelling cinnamon, make sure you hold it far enough away that you are not breathing in the actual particles, as this will cause you to sneeze. If it is an orange, scratch the surface of the peeling slightly to allow the fragrance to be released, so you get the "zest" of its scent.

- Breathe this in and let it permeate your sense of being, feeling a soothing, calming sensation.

- Take this feeling with you as you prepare your meal.

Going Inward Before the Meal

What did you sense when you took the time to feel and smell what you chose? Identify one essence that came to the surface. Keep alive in your mind what essence came up for you. You are now ready to bring the energy of that essence to your cooking and the Table of Life.

_____

_____

_____

_____

Zoe's Fun Fruity Nutty Salad

As I mentioned above, Zoe, my youngest granddaughter, loves to play Chopped, and is so very creative and artistic. She loves fruit and all things sweet, so this recipe reflects her personality: fun, fruity and nutty! ENJOY!

Serves 4
Prep time: 25 minutes

Ingredients

2 navel seedless oranges, peeled & cut into small bite size pieces
1 cup pineapple, peeled, cored & chopped
1 mango, peeled & chopped
4 organic kiwis, peeled, & chopped
12 Lg. organic strawberries, chopped
½ cup organic blueberries
1 ½ cups organic raspberries
¼ cup orange juice
¼ cup lemon juice
4 sprigs chopped mint
2 Tbs slivered roasted almonds*
1 Tbs chia seed
1 Tbs hemp seeds

Method

Who doesn't love fruit? Enjoy the process of looking at all the different colors, touching the different textures, chopping, cutting, smelling and peeling every delicious piece of fruit.

Chop all of the fruits as mentioned above.

Get a big, big bowl, even if the ingredients don't fill up the bowl entirely, so you have plenty of room to mix without thinking about spilling it over.

As you are cutting and chopping, smell the fragrance from each fruit and let your eyes delight in the multi-colors you are creating.

If you can't eat nuts, leave them out, but I have to say, they are a nice addition to the crunch factor while savoring each bite.

Mix everything together and enjoy!

You can even add a dollop of whip cream on the top for the fun of it!

Going Inward After the Meal

Smelling is an important sense that we have as human beings. It's the second to last sense to go before we die. Hearing is the last sense. Take a moment to write what essence you discovered through the sense of smell exercise. How did that affect your cooking experience? Were you more aware of smelling each ingredient that you used? Did you let yourself take in the aromas and fill yourself up with feelings of well-being? What takeaways did you discover in your essence you brought through this Happy Mindful Meditation?

Self-Reflections/Notes

Conclusion

I hope you've enjoyed your taste of Soul-Diving™, as well as discovering and even re-acquainting yourself with some of your unique essences. There's a different awareness of what you bring to the Table of Life once you are consciously aware of 'who-you-are-while-you-are-cooking'. The whole endeavor of this book was to inspire you to bring up and re-acquaint yourself with those essences that are unique to you in how they manifest themselves. You may choose to have this book serve as your savory, sensory and inspirational guide to discover your own unique essences that lead you to live a yummy delicious life, regardless of whatever may be going on in your environment.

New perspectives, tools, tips and Re-*Minders* may even serve as new ways of looking at the ingredients that make up the recipe of your life.

The *Happy Mindful Meditations* are designed to inspire a habit of giving yourself a few moments of BEing in peace and quiet prior to cooking. It's just a short "time-out" that reconnects you with your essences. I believe that this method of BEing in conscious awareness will prove to be of great benefit to you.

My hope is that all you have read, has touched your heart, motivated you, and sparked your mind to engage in enriching the quality of your life. In doing so, you put yourself first, acknowledging that you are your own CEO (Chief Energy Officer). Know that your energy sends "vibes", and when you are in the habit of BEing calmly consistent, others around you will absorb that. The entire experience of preparing, cooking and serving up your dishes are metaphors for serving up life experiences.

All the essences that you have either discovered or re-acquainted yourself with, are what you bring to your environment, and can become even your legacy. Unique essences of you that have touched other's hearts, and have inspired them in some way, will be what others will always remember – these essences in action have the power to change someone's life. First and foremost, it's to deepen the quality of your own life for a more joyful one – regardless of what is going on around you.

This book was also intended to show you that no matter what your early environment life was like, you can reframe thoughts and paradigms so that they serve you towards a more wonderful life, with a feeling of well-being and one of being blessed. You will engage in bringing what you want and need to your table, and thus to the Table of Life.

In taking a deeper stock of your true essences, you can remove or add a few ingredients until you get the "right" sweet and savory balance you need to live a fulfilling, meaningful and joyful life.

We are human and we may make mistakes, however, forgiveness must be part of the deal, so you can unconditionally love yourself up, and trust that all is well. You have a feeling that the Universe/Nature/God/All That Is/Love has got your back, because you are made up of the same energy that everything else is made up of, that there is no separation. Remember that love is the most healing elixir and one of the most precious yummy delicious essences you get to bring to the Table of Life. Feel it. Spread it. Share it.

Your life quality is an inside job, that finding joy and sustaining it takes practice, that's it's your responsibility, no matter how much you want to give the baton of power to someone else. You're worth the time and energy you invest in yourself. My wish is for you to eat the slices of life with a side of well-being. Continue to take a look at how much time you spend in areas you don't want vs areas you want. Remember to focus on what you want so that you find the essences you wish to bring forth, shedding light on your abilities, skills and talents and radiating them out to the world.

May you be and stay present in every possible moment, so that you become aware of what thoughts are running you, allowing yourself to shift your thinking to have more pleasant experiences in whatever you do. Just be conscious of your thoughts, words, tone and actions. When you are heart-driven you are reformulating the familiar formula that has been running your mind, creating new and healthy neural pathways that lead you to living the life you want, increasing your Joy Factor, knowing that you can change generational patterns once and for all. When you live from an authentic place, you become more loving, kind and compassionate.

When you have a healthy relationship with yourself, you are more apt to have a healthy relationship with others, feeling confident that whatever you have to share comes from the heart and that you are able to hold the space for others to have their human experience without judgment. Remember the three "F" words, Forgiveness, Fingerpointyitus, and Friends for Life. Each one of these concepts helps you to navigate your human experience with more compassion, understanding and patience.

Also remember that love is the ultimate emotion that has the ability to heal. When you bring love into the equation, it sets a tone that is kind, thoughtful, caring and understanding, as it ignites, inspires and is a catalyst for more love. I believe you can't ever have too much love. Love = Energy and Spirit, for when you feel it, you feel connected and you create an inner coherence within your own physical body and with other cosmic bodies. When you allow, you accept that you are part of everything. You get to surrender and just "be" without being influenced by how others want you to live.

When you create a beautiful environment, with everything in it that reflects love, you are giving yourself permission to live in beauty, a reflection of your heart. Soaking in your natural juices of wellbeing permeates your inner sanctuary with feelings of sincerity and sweet joy. I hope that you see how you can live mindfully happy with love from your heart, able to connect in ways that you appreciate your own one-of-a-kind unique self.

Remembering that changing your thoughts definitely changes your life, tells your brain to secrete the particular chemicals that are based on the thoughts you think. When you are able to change the thoughts into healthier ones, your life changes, because your body is no longer in control. It's as simple as that, and when you share with the people you love, well, you feel connected with yourself and with others. Then, it's practice time to sustain and maintain that delicious sense of well-being, becoming a role model for living your legacy, so that you can pass on your values to the next generation. Once you identify the values you want to live, then you can contribute to the world in a new and exciting way, paying it forward and living your life fully with honor, dignity and regard.

Thank you for taking your time to read this book. It was definitely written with love from my heart to yours.

I would love to hear some of your favorite take-aways from what you have read, and any "AHA" moments that made you say, "Hmmm, I never looked at it that way (whatever the "it" was). That's very interesting." Please email me at shelleywhiz@gmail.com I look forward to hearing your thoughts.

Take care. It's your life. Enjoy the journey. And remember to bring love into everything you do.

Many blessings,

Shelley

Self-Reflections/Notes

Review of Bite Size Re-Minders to Living a Yummy Delicious Life

Chapter 1: Preparation of Self – Getting into the Deep-Dive

- I remember to take time out, quiet the inner chatter and find my inner calm.

- I remember when I take time out for myself, I am honoring myself.

- I remember to BE present and let myself enjoy my experience.

- I remember to be conscious of my breath throughout the day.

- I remember I am the CEO (Chief Energy Officer) of my own life.

Chapter 2: Energy – The Boundless Spirit

- I remember that my energy is part of the same particles and waves of the boundless Universe.

- I remember that my thoughts are also made up of the same living energy as the foods we eat and impact the way in which I live.

- I remember I that energy can be changed from one form to another, but never destroyed.

- I remember that I am able to transform my thoughts from one form to another, by changing my perspective.

- I remember that being "disturbed" or "heated" up is an important ingredient to my growth as a human being.

Chapter 3: Heart-Driven: The Joy Factor

- I remember when I come from love and am heart-driven I am rewiring my brain, creating coherence, and over time, this pattern becomes the norm.
- I remember it takes practice and time to marinate in the right formula.
- I remember to let go of negative thoughts before I cook.
- I remember that I am responsible for my life.
- I remember to live in the moment and be present NOW.

Chapter 4: Relationships: Family & Friends for Life

- I remember to nourish my relationships, starting with the one I have with my Self.
- I remember never to pry someone's heart open if they don't want it opened.
- I remember to accept other people's perspective and hold the space for them to have their human experience without judgment.
- I remember to forgive others and myself for being human and making mistakes.
- I remember to not point the finger out and blame others for how I feel and to take full responsibility for what I am experiencing.

Chapter 5: Love, Love, Love

- I remember that love is the magic healing elixir, standing the test of time.
- I remember to bring love into everything I do.
- I remember to allow myself to be loving, loveable and loved.
- I remember that love IS the energy that grows all things, beats our hearts and breathes our bodies.

- I remember that love is the gift that keeps on giving.

Chapter 6: Creating your Sanctuary

- I remember that my home is a reflection of my heart. I will only bring in objects that I love.
- I remember my home is my sanctuary, a place of comfort, solace and support.
- I remember to let go of any object that carries negative energy.
- I remember that I deserve to live in a loving environment.
- I remember to have fun in my own home, that it is a place of joy.

Chapter 7: Change your Thoughts, Change your Life

- I remember not to take myself too seriously.
- I remember I what I put my attention on my energy flows.
- I remember to be conscious of my thoughts.
- I remember to pay attention to my thought patterns and focus on what I want instead of what I don't want.
- I remember that my energy and thoughts are made up of the same waves and particles that the Universe is made up of.

Chapter 8: Connecting - Sharing and Caring

- I remember to bring the importance of connecting with my body, mind and spirit, building a true connection between my human and my soul.
- I remember to bring love, joy and fun to whatever I do.

- I remember that if I am "trying" to connect with someone by "being interesting, funny or smart," I am looking for other people's reactions, rather than authentically sharing or caring.

- I remember to bring a kind word to and about others, that gossiping with others is not truly connecting, it's just talking about someone with disrespect.

- I remember when I do something for someone, I do out of sincerity, no guilt or obligation.

Chapter 9: A New Way of BEing

- I remember to open my heart and be grateful.

- I remember to nurture my relationship between my imagination, my heart and soul.

- I remember to fill myself up with positive experiences and let myself feel the elevated emotions.

- I remember that it's okay to imagine what I want and who I want to be and let myself HAVE the experience in the moment.

- I remember that I am worth changing my thoughts and my life for, that I deserve to live a happy, joyous life with a sense of well-being.

Chapter 10: BEing Your Legacy

- I remember that a human being's life journey is very much like a butterfly's life, valuable, fleeting, and beautiful.

- I remember to believe in my own self-worth and know that my presence is of utmost value.

- I remember I have an effect on others, no matter how "minor" I think it is, it has long lasting effects, whether I am conscious of it or not.
- I remember I am a one-of-a-kind unique human being and have my own gifts to give to others
- I remember that I am a living legacy.

Chapter 11: Contributing to the World

- I remember that coming from the heart, with love and care for others is a way of contributing to the world.
- I remember to be kind, thoughtful and genuinely interested in others, as a way of contributing to the world.
- I remember to be conscious of what I bring to the Table of Life, whether volunteering my skills, my talents or my time, that I am contributing to the world.
- I remember that even in the small gestures, I am contributing to the world.
- I remember it's in the giving that the receiving takes place, not in the expectation of getting.

Glossary of Shelley's Terms

Word	Definition
A Dash	A small quantity of a substance added to something else. Use your instinct to add a dash of this or that.
Add	Joining something to something else to increase the amount, increase your joy factor.
Appetite	A natural desire to satisfy a bodily need, especially for food, an inherent craving an insatiable - a strong desire or liking for something - the desire to eat food or have an appetite for living life experiences.
Aroma/Aromatic	The smell of something yummy delicious cooking, the flavorful scent of having a wonderful time.
Baking	The practice or skill of preparing food by combining, mixing, and heating ingredients, baking up an idea, heating it up until it's ready.
Basting	Pouring juices or melted fat over (meat) during cooking in order to keep it moist, keeping an idea fresh and ready.
Better	An uplifting feeling that lifts us from a place that felt bad to a new place where change is felt towards strength = progress, improvement from where we were to where we are.

Bite-size pieces	Digestible pieces of information that we can assimilate when we are ready.
Bitter-sweet	Sweet with a bitter aftertaste. Arousing pleasure tinged with sadness or pain, a growing experience.
Blending	The action of mixing or combining things together. Mix of ideas and thoughts that reflect an open-minded approach to life.
Boil/Boiling	The action of bringing a liquid to the temperature at which it bubbles and turns to vapor. When energy heats up enough it changes form.
Breath	The inhalation and exhalation from the lungs, the life force that animates you, that keeps you alive, that helps you to be and stay present.
Breathing in the Fragrance of life	Taking in all the sweetness of living and making it yours.
Candied	Preserve (fruit) by coating and impregnating it with a sugar syrup, sugar coating an experience.
CEO Chief Energy Officer	You are the one in charge of your own energy. You are the manager of your own life.
Chaos to order	Cooking is like a puzzle with pieces to put together.
Condiment	A substance such as salt or ketchup that is used to add flavor to food. Adding flavor to the experiences we have.
Consommé	A clear soup made with concentrated stock. When we have the essence, we can build from there.

Consume	Eat, drink or ingest food or drink; buy; use up; completely destroy; consumed: feeling absorbed all of the attention and energy of someone. Taking in your own energy of life.
Cooking	The practice or skill of preparing food by combining, mixing, and heating ingredients. One can cook up a storm in the kitchen or in life, depending on the ingredients and intentions used.
Craving	A powerful desire for something, it could be food or an experience or an emotion, a yearning.
Creaming	Work (two or more ingredients, typically butter and sugar) together to form a creamy paste. When you want to experience something creamy, mixing two qualities of life that merge effortlessly.
Delectable	Delicious, agreeable, blessed, delightful, enjoyable, gratifying, heavenly, palatable, pleasant, pleasurable, savory, sweet, tasty, welcome. Having an exquisite life experience that you can just taste with delight.
Delicious	Highly pleasant to the taste. It is just yummy all the way around!
Digestion	The process of breaking down food by mechanical and enzymatic action in the alimentary canal into substances that can be used by the body. When we want to digest certain principles in life, it takes a process of digestion to break them down into pieces that are absorbed into our system.
Dip	A thick sauce in which pieces of food are dunked before eating. We can dip into ideas here and there too.

Doting	Loving up with sincere warmth and generousness
Dressing	A sauce for salads, typically one consisting of oil and vinegar mixed together with herbs or other flavorings. You can dress up your life with wonderful experiences, mixing this and that together. Have fun dressing your life!
Easy	Simple recipe that are easy to follow. Doing life effortlessly. Uncomplicated, calm, tranquil, serene, quiet, peaceful. When you are heart-centered, you bring a sense of ease and grace into every situation.
Effervescent	Giving off bubbles, fizzy; vivacious and enthusiastic. Expressing an appealing lively quality.
Embellish	Make something more attractive by adding decorative details or features, making something more interesting or entertaining by adding extra details, especially ones that may not be true. Adding to whatever you do in a beautiful way.
Energy	Exists in many forms, such as heat, light, chemical energy, and electrical energy. Energy is the ability to bring about change or to do work. Thermodynamics is the study of energy.
Enjoy	Take delight or pleasure in (an activity or occasion); having a pleasant time. Appreciate, like, love, revel in, savor, adore, eat up, get a kick out of, etc. There are so many words that reflect enjoyment, it's time to have fun in whatever you do. Do whatever you do for the fun of it.

Epigenetics	The study of genes and DNA, most often involving changes that affect gene activity and expression. Dr. Bruce Lipton is a leading researcher showing how genes are altered by the thoughts that we think, therefore proving that thoughts can change the pre-disposition of inherited genes, disproving that we are victims, doomed to live out what our ancestors passed onto us.
Essence	A concentrated energy that describes the very heart and soul of nature, whether it's food or life values.
Feed	Give food, eat something; provide an adequate supply of; derive regular nourishment from a particular substance; give fertilizer to a plant; encourage the growth of; give nourishment to your own body, mind heart and soul's experience of YOU.
Filter	A porous device for removing impurities or solid particles from a liquid or gas passed through it; life experiences that one uses to determine the reaction or response given.
Fingerpointyitus	Disease in blaming someone else for how you feel, for your state of being, pointing the finger out. Remember when you are pointing the finger out, there are still 3 fingers pointing back at yourself.
Flambé	Covered with liquor and set aflame briefly. Lighting an old thought pattern on fire to get your attention.
Flavor	The distinctive taste of a food or drink. It's the taste in your mouth from your life experience.

Flavoring	A substance used to give a different, stronger, or more agreeable taste to food or drink
Flourish	Grow or develop in a healthy or vigorous way, especially as the result of a particularly favorable environment.
Fold	Bend (something flexible and relatively flat) over on itself so that one part of it covers another. When you fold experiences into our life turn them with love.
Formula	A list of ingredients for or constituents of something. When you create a formula for your life that works, be mindful of the ingredients and keep them active.
Fresh	Recently made or obtained, not canned, frozen or otherwise preserved; not previously known or used, new or different; recently created or experienced, not faded or impaired; person attractively youthful and inexperienced; full of energy and vigor. Add a fresh perspective to your life.
Happenstance	Living life according to what "happens" to us by chance and reacting accordingly depending on what belief you carry.
Healthy	Being sound and well; not sick; showing good health a healthy complexion; aiding or building up health healthy exercise; rather large in extent or amount. It's important to have healthy thoughts for a healthy lifestyle.

Heat	The quality of being hot, high temperature, form of energy arising from random motion of the molecules of bodies, which may be transferred by conduction, convection or radiation; spicy quality in food; heat needed to cause a specific process of transformation; intensity of feeling especially of anger or excitement.
Humble	The adoption of humility as a strength/not weakness.
Indulgent	Willing to allow excessive leniency, generosity, or consideration; indulging or characterized by indulgence; done or enjoyed as a special treat or pleasure indulgent desserts. Indulging in your life's joy is a good thing.
Ingredients	Any of the foods or substances that are combined to make a particular dish. Look at all the ingredients you can add in your life. They are abundant.
Instinct Cooking	An innate, intuitive way of acting or thinking, relying on your own intuition for making food; the fact or quality of possessing innate behavior patterns. Trust yourself.
Joy	A feeling of great pleasure that is bound to a sense of well-being from the inside out and doesn't depend on circumstance.
Joy Factor Scale	The level of joy one lives from 1, being miserable/ discontent to 10, being utterly joyful.
Juicy	Full of juice; succulent, tasty, scrumptious. Having a juicy conversation with someone you care about is the best!

Law of Thermodynamics	Energy can be changed from one form to another, but it cannot be created or destroyed. The total amount of energy and matter in the Universe remains constant, merely changing from one form to another. Love never dies.
Loved up	Doted upon with genuineness and heart = Love.
Main Course	The most substantial course of a meal = your Life.
Marinate	Soak (meat, fish, or other food) in a marinade; steep in, bask in, bathe in, take in. When you marinate in your own sense of well-being, it permeates everything you do.
Measure	Ascertain the size, amount, or degree of (something) by using an instrument or device marked in standard units or by comparing it with an object of known size. You can measure your own joy factor by how you feel.
Mindful	Focusing one's awareness on the present moment, especially as part of a therapeutic or meditative technique. Bringing yourself into the present moment by being conscious of where you are, how you feel and what you are doing.
Mix	Combine or put together to form one substance or mass. You can mix your life up with experiences of all kinds.
Mouthwatering	Smelling, looking, or sounding delicious - highly attractive or tempting. When you have a mouthwatering experience, you never forget it. The taste lasts a long time.

Natural	Existing in or caused by nature; not made or caused by humankind. When you are yourself and come from the heart, you are being the way you were meant to be. YOU!
Nourish/Nourishing	Provide food or other substances necessary for growth, health and good condition; keep a feeling or belief in one's mind, typically for a long time, nourishing the body, mind, heart and soul.
Organic	Relating to or derived from living matter. Do yourself a favor and use organic produce as much as possible.
Palate	The roof of the mouth, separating the cavities of the nose and the mouth in vertebrates - a person's appreciation of taste and flavor, especially when sophisticated and discriminating. When you have a certain palate/taste, you want more of it.
Pinch	A smidgen, a little, just enough to add a particular flavor or enhance a flavor that's already there. When you add a pinch of grace to your life, it feels easier.
Portion	A part of a whole, something divided between two or more people; an amount of food suitable for or served to one person. Sharing your portions with others is a wonderful way to live life.
Pour	Cause to flow from a container, prepare and serve; express one's feelings or thoughts in a full and unrestrained way; feeling safe to pour out your feelings with another.

Precision	The quality, condition, or fact of being exact and accurate. In some recipes this may be needed but use your instincts.
Pungent	Having a sharply strong taste or smell. Rely on your sense of smell to guide you when cooking or living for that matter.
Quantum soup	The quantum is filled with potential energy that we are all part of. Each of us is a particular ingredient made up of particles and waves, where anything is possible.
Raw	Uncooked, material in its natural state, not yet processed or purified. When you have raw emotions, examine where they come from.
Recipes	A set of instructions for preparing a particular dish, including a list of the ingredients required. You make up the recipe of your own life, depending on the ingredients you use.
Reduce	Make smaller or less in amount, degree or size; boil in cooking so that it becomes thicker and more concentrated. You can reduce your stress levels by changing your thoughts.
Refresh/Refreshing	Give new strength or energy to; reinvigorate; stimulate or jog someone's memory; revise or update skills or knowledge; pour more drink for someone; place or keep food in cold water so as to cool or maintain freshness. Refresh your mind.
Relish	A condiment eaten with plain food to add flavor – great enjoyment. Relish your life in all ways.

Rich	Having valuable natural resources; plentiful, abundant, having a large amount, containing a large amount of fat, spices, sugar, etc.; full bodied; producing a large quantity of something. Be rich in love.
Satiated	Satisfied to the full; as one's appetite or desire. Enjoy being satisfied until your next desire takes you on another journey.
Sauce	Thick liquid served with food, usually savory dishes, to add moistness and flavor. Sometimes when we add a "sauce" to our lives, it becomes spicy and fun!
Sauté'	Fry quickly in a little hot fat. Don't be afraid to dance a hot little dance in your living room when no one is watching.
Savor	Taste (good food or drink) and enjoy it completely - a characteristic taste, flavor, or smell, especially a pleasant one - Whether it's a feeling of joy or a piece of pecan pie. When you savor something, you enjoy it to the fullest. Enjoy it.
Savory	Belonging to the category that is salty or spicy rather than sweet - morally wholesome or acceptable. Very tasty experiences that last.
Science	The intellectual and practical activity encompassing the systematic study of the structure and behavior of the physical and natural world through observation and experiment. Science is the contemporary language for spirituality.

Seasoning	Salt, herbs, or spices added to food to enhance the flavor. Always feel free to add your favorite seasonings to your life.
Servings	A quantity of food suitable for or served to one person. Always make more and give it away. It's so gratifying.
Side Dish	A dish served as a subsidiary to the main one. Adding side dish experiences to your life deepen the quality of living.
Sieve	A utensil consisting of a wire or plastic mesh held in a frame, used for straining solids from liquids, for separating coarser from finer particles, or for reducing soft solids to a pulp. Just like life to refine the thoughts that no longer serve you.
Simmer	Stay just below the boiling point while being heated. Sometimes you need to let your thoughts simmer before responding.
Sizzle	Make a hissing sound when frying or cooking. It's a treat for your ears and so satisfying to hear food sizzling in a pan.
Slow	Burning or giving off heat gently. When we allow ourselves to slow down and be present, it builds a sense of patience.
Smell	The faculty or power of perceiving odors or scents by means of the organs in the nose - perceive or detect the odor or scent of (something). Use your sense of smell to delight, engage and guide you in your own life.

Soak	Make or allow something to become thoroughly wet by immersing it in liquid; cause something to become extremely wet; a liquid that penetrates or permeates completely. Sometimes we have to let ourselves soak in a thought to repattern our mind.
Soul Diving	A process of diving into yourself to discover your own sense of being through self-reflection, looking at the human experience through the soul's perspective.
Space	A continuous area or expanse which is free, available or unoccupied; a blank between printed, typed or written words, characters, numbers, etc.; the dimension of height, depth and width within which all things exist and move; the physical universe beyond the earth's atmosphere and within every cell of our being. Being conscious of space helps us to expand.
Spice	An aromatic or pungent vegetable substance used to flavor food, e.g., cloves, pepper, cinnamon, curry. Spicing up our life with new thoughts grows our awareness of new ways of being.
Spiritual	Relating to or affecting the human spirit or soul as opposed to material or physical things. Spiritual = Energy, the life force that animates our body and life.
Spoiled	Food becoming unfit for eating; person harmed in character by being treated too leniently or indulgently. Trust your instincts when something doesn't feel right.

Stew	A dish of meat and vegetables cooked slowly in liquid in a closed dish or pan; informal worry about something, especially on one's own; be steeped in or imbued with (stew in one's own juice: suffer anxiety or the unpleasant consequences of one's own actions without the consoling intervention of others). Sometimes we just have to stew before we can realize what we are stewing about.
Stir	Move a spoon or other implement around in (a liquid or other substance) in order to mix it thoroughly. - a commotion. When you stir up commotion, you are releasing the stuck particles at the bottom, bringing them up to the surface to either skim off or mix back in a different way.
Sustaining	To provide with what is needed to stay in a certain state; food sustains life. When you are able to sustain a sense of well-being and joy, there is nothing that you cannot face in life with grace by your side.
Sustenance	Food or drink regarded as a source of strength; nourishment; maintaining of someone or something in life of existence. The sustenance of love permeates every action with kindness, honor, regard and dignity.
Sweet	Having the pleasant taste characteristic of sugar or honey; not salty, sour, or bitter; an experience that brings a sense of well-being and joy.

Sweet & Sour	Sweet and sour is used to describe both a sweet flavor and something sharp or sour such as lemon or vinegar. Sometimes there are sweet and sour experiences in life and that is part of the human experience.
Tangy	Having a strong, piquant flavor or smell. Bring it!
Taste	The sensation of flavor perceived in the mouth and throat on contact with a substance - a person's liking for particular flavors. Everyone's taste is different. Rely on your own. It's yours.
Tasty	Food having a pleasant, distinct flavor; very attractive or appealing. Kissing can be a very tasty and enjoyable experience.
Torch	To set afire, portable means of illumination, such as a piece of wood or cloth; used to refer to a valuable quality, principle or cause, that needs to be protected and maintained; set fire to. Sometimes thoughts and beliefs need to be torched to get our attention.
Unfold	To open or undo something folded or make something known that wasn't. When we allow our lives to unfold, we allow the universe to guide us on our way without effort.
Unrefined	Not processed to remove impurities or unwanted elements - in a natural state, without having been through a chemical or industrial process to remove. Be in your natural state.

Well-being	An overriding feel of safety, that all is okay and will be okay. The state of being comfortable, healthy, or happy - the state of being joyful, healthy, or prosperous.
Whip	A dessert consisting of cream or eggs beaten into a light fluffy mass with fruit, chocolate, or other ingredients; a utensil such as a whisk or an eggbeater for beating cream, eggs, or other food. Whipping your life with ingredients that you desire will give you what you desire.
Whisk	Beat or stir (a substance, especially cream or eggs) with a light, rapid movement. Letting yourself feel excited and calm at the same time.
Wholesome	Conducive to or suggestive of good health and physical well-being - conducive to or promoting health or well-being of mind, body or spirit. An all-around good feeling.
Yummy	Delicious - delicious food - highly attractive or pleasing especially delicious, delectable yummy desserts; a feeling of great satisfaction and contentment.
Yummy Delicious	Feeling good inside; warm & fuzzy; inspired, grateful, overall feeling of well-being, joyful, happy.
Zest	Great enthusiasm and energy - the outer colored part of the peel of citrus fruit, used as flavoring. Zest up your life!

More Acknowledgements

Susan Rosenthal, from World Global Markets, "Thank you, Susan, for the inspirational visions you shared with me for this book." 🙏

I thank Robert Martinez from Manifestation Technology for his astuteness and direction to further grow some aspects related to my book and future projects. "Robert, you're my friend for life, I appreciate your genius so very much, as well as your devotion and invaluable input." 🙏

I also want to acknowledge all those special individuals who have trusted themselves to seek guidance from me, allowing me to step right into their hearts. I am happy for you, and I feel honored that you chose me to be the catalyst to transform your life. I hold a deep regard for you and never take lightly the commitment to elevate and deepen the quality of your life's journey. 🙏

I want to acknowledge Regina Rosa, my best friend since I was 13 years old. It seems like yesterday that we rode our skateboards together and bought that one-way ticket to Europe when we were just 19. "My life is always an adventure with you, Regina. Thank you for the levity and the belly laughs that last for hours on end. You are truly my sister and my first friend for life." 🙏

I am thankful to have my two delightfully charming lady cheerleaders and friends for life by my side, Diana Ferguson and Christinea Johnson. "Together, we continue the journey into the enlightening study of our human/spiritual dynamic together for thirty-six years. Thank you for providing me with such heartfelt support." 🙏

"Olivia Bareham, your sensitive nature is so endearing. I love how open you are to continue to learn about this human experience, and I feel so blessed to count you as my friend for life. How you help families transition through the end of life experience is exquisite." 🙏

"Dannion Brinkley, finding The Twilight Brigade and becoming a national trainer, gave me wonderful perspectives on life. Thank you for trusting me with the souls of all the students I have trained – the course is truly life-changing." 🙏

"Roger Love – watching you grow into a fine, talented, giving, and brilliant light in this world of ours, has been/is/will always be such a pleasure. Thank you for believing in me, and for showing such great enthusiasm for encouraging me to use my voice in writing this book." 🙏

"Darsweil Rogers, I am forever grateful that you became an instant friend for life from day one. You have continually invigorated me with our deep and stimulating conversations about BEing human, exploring together how it applies to every field, including the corporate world. Thank you for having me on your radio show and for the hours of such great conversations. You always bring a joyous smile to my face."

I want to acknowledge and thank Bruce Whizin, who has always encouraged me to write. "My life is full of blessings because of you, Bruce. I thank you for the love that will always be."

I'd like to acknowledge two very special people who I was fortunate enough to be friends with for life, my beautiful friends Toni and Gene Bua. Their gifts of inspiration are with me in everything I do. "May you soar with the angels."

I would not be here if it were not for my parents, Ruth and Al Silver (both of blessed memory). From both of them I learned how to be, and how not to be in this world. I learned how to dance the jitterbug from my dad, and I learned how to cook and clean from my, mom. My house is immaculate, full of music. and my life is full of love.

I thank my sisters Judy Karni, Andrea Stoltzman, and Lani Silver, along with my brother Ron Silver and his wife, Cindy, and my younger brother Mark Silver (of blessed memory), and Alec Stoltzman, (also of blessed memory), and all of my nieces/grandnieces and nephews, Blake, Shane, Emily, Dahlia, David, Aaron, Daniel, Jacob, Rebekah, Yael, Maddy, and Oren, with Juliette in tow, for your tenacity to be the best you can be, and for your humor. Thank God we got dad's humor.

Last but not least, I thank my Papa Rosa for showing me the strength it takes to go through the Holocaust and still be Superman at 95 years old. "You are my hero, Papa. I thank you for loving me over the years, and I admire you so much for teaching the next generations about life through your own life story of being a Holocaust Survivor." 🙏

More Endorsements

*"At this time in history this jewel **"What You Bring to The Table"** comes to us to help wake us up to our true selves. More than ever, the valuable concepts and teachings in this book are timely for everything we are experiencing each in our way, and on a worldwide level. Shelley takes us brilliantly on a Deep Dive into ourselves and makes us aware that every thought can be transmuted into something that can feel good or less than good. It cannot only affect the taste of the food and how it goes into our tummies, but also, how we are nurtured. We are aware that we can get still, breathe and meditate, and shift the thought to each come up with an essence. Then this feeling and essence we carry into the preparation of our food making the taste enhanced by it and stands to fuel us into an even greater experience."*

-Kerri Leblang, Author, Actress, Songwriter, Singer, Writer

*"Reading your lovely cookbook '**What do you Bring to the Table**' was so delightful, and I could almost hear your voice in every word I read. There are too many areas to list that I liked in this book, but Chapter 3 and 4 were special highlights for me (I also tried your meatloaf recipe. Yum!) Chapter 7 provided me with another deeper layer of personal insights. I love the format that was created, and the "Bite Size Reminders" are fantastic for quick reference. The Happy Mindful Meditations are great, and I truly love how they are tied into food and the "ingredients" we bring to the table of life. The section that's provided for writing down your essence and reflections on our experience after doing the Meditation, as well as "Going Inward After the Meal", were perfect for me! I'm buying several copies of your book to give away to many of my close friends. They all love food and like to cook so that will be a way to resonate with your teachings about what we each can bring to the table of life."*

-Tracy Korf

I learned so much from this book. It really made me look at things differently and think about things in a different way. One of the biggest things that stood out to me was that if I change my thoughts, I can allow myself to imagine the future/what I wish to happen. Also, I never realized that I needed to bring love and passion into making food. Sometimes, I just want to make something quick because I am hungry and don't feel like cooking. Now, I know that if I cook with love it makes the food taste so much better and it makes me feel better. You made me think of so many things differently that I positively would not have thought on my own. I know what it means to give back to the world and expect nothing in return, as well as to do good deeds out of the goodness of my heart. I'm so proud of you Noons, this is an amazing book!

-Jordyn Schultz, Granddaughter, 14 years old

About the Author

Shelley Whizin is an inspirational guide of light by nature, and the Founder of the Soul Diving Institute™, established to provide courses, workshops and personalized coaching on the "art and science of BEing human." It is through the process of Soul Diving that helps people navigate their human experience with as much ease and grace as possible, finding a sense of well-being to live a happy, mindful, empowered, and heart-driven life.

Shelley is a life-long learner and teacher of the human-spiritual connection. Her desire to understand the spiritual nature of BEing human, led her to travel the world studying shamanism in Peru and Ecuador; ancient Toltec traditions in Mexico; Eastern traditions and philosophies of Hinduism, Buddhism and Christianity in India, and Jewish culture and life in Israel, along with mysticism and religious studies with rabbis, thought leaders and teachers in the U.S., including earning a bachelor's degree in Jewish studies when she was fifty, Suma Cum Laude. Later, her search for a contemporary language for spirituality led Shelley to add neuroscience, quantum physics, epigenetics, hypnosis, and neurological repatterning (NLP) to her knowledge and toolbox.

Being a guider of light, fueled by a deep compassion and care for others, Shelley holds the intention to heal life experiences with love, honor and dignity. Shelley's immense value draws from certifications and experiences as a life coach, motivational speaker, course facilitator, yoga instructor, hospice trainer and death midwife. Among her many courses Shelley has developed, one of her favorites is

"Instinct Cooking", her proprietary approach to cooking from the inside out. Shelley lives in Sherman Oaks, CA, a quick "meal's distance" from her daughter and three creatively gifted grandchildren.

Contact Information

Email: Shelleywhiz@gmail.com

Shelley's Assistant
ShelleyAsst@gmail.com

What Do You Bring to the Table? Website:
www.whatdoyoubringtothetablebook.com

Soul Diving Institute Website:
www.souldivinginstitute.com

Instagram
https://www.instagram.com/shelleywhizin/?hl=en

Personal Facebook
https://www.facebook.com/shelley.whizin

Soul Diving Facebook
https://www.facebook.com/Shelley.S.Whizin/

Twitter
https://twitter.com/shelleywhiz

LinkedIn
https://www.linkedin.com/in/shelleywhizin/

CPSIA information can be obtained
at www.ICGtesting.com
Printed in the USA
LVHW011125291220
675071LV00009B/1097

9 781087 932101